The New York Times

LOOKING FORWARD

Disruptive Innovation

UBER, AIRBNB AND OTHER COMPANIES RESHAPING THE MARKET

EDUCATIONAL PUBLISHING BOOKS

I0878998

THE NEW YORK TIMES EDITORIAL STAFF

Published in 2019 by New York Times Educational Publishing in association with The Rosen Publishing Group, Inc.
29 East 21st Street, New York, NY 10010

First Edition

The New York Times
Alex Ward: Editorial Director, Book Development
Brenda Hutchings: Senior Photo Editor/Art Buyer
Phyllis Collazo: Photo Rights/Permissions Editor
Heidi Giovine: Administrative Manager

Rosen Publishing
Greg Tucker: Creative Director
Brian Garvey: Art Director
Megan Kellerman: Managing Editor
Carolyn DeCarlo: Editor

Cataloging-in-Publication Data
Names: New York Times Company.
Title: Disruptive innovation: Uber, Airbnb and other companies reshaping the market / edited by the New York Times editorial staff.
Description: New York : The New York Times Educational Publishing, 2019. | Series: Looking forward | Includes glossary and index.
Identifiers: ISBN 9781642820805 (pbk.) | ISBN 9781642820812 (library bound) | ISBN 9781642820829 (ebook)
Subjects: LCSH: Business enterprises—Juvenile literature. | New business enterprises—Juvenile literature. | Sharing—Economic aspects—Juvenile literature
Classification: LCC HB615.D577 2019 | DDC 658.1'1—dc23

Manufactured in the United States of America

On the cover: Drones at Hannan General Aviation Airport in Wuhan, China; Lam Yik Fei for The New York Times.

Contents

CHAPTER 2

Transportation

CHAPTER 3

Blockchain and Cryptocurrencies

CHAPTER 5

Smart Homes and the Internet of Things

Introduction

WHAT DO UBER, self-driving cars, gene editing, bitcoin, and Amazon Echo have in common? They are all drivers of disruptive innovation.

Coined by Harvard professor and businessman Clayton Christensen, the term "disruptive innovation" describes the evolution of a service or product that changes the market. Usually created by start-up companies, disruptive innovation is designed to capture a new customer base and, in the process, change the way companies and consumers behave. While behavior-changing disruption has existed for as long as humans have, the technological revolution of the late 20th century inexorably shaped disruptive innovation.

In the early 1970s, Martin Cooper, an engineer at Motorola, designed the first handheld cell phone. His idea was that calls could be made directly to a person rather than to a place. Nearly fifty years later, the ubiquitous use of cell phones has rendered traditional landline phones nearly obsolete. Apple's touchscreen smartphone then turned the cell phone into a handheld computer. One device replaced users' cameras, video recorders, web browsers, email software, navigational systems, streaming entertainment players and watches.

Amazon's powerful online shopping platform gave consumers an easy way to find, compare prices on, order and have what they wanted delivered to their homes — and now in 30 minutes by drone — at a low cost. Called "the Amazon effect," the subsequent change in consumer behavior forced other retailers to offer online purchasing options, and many have since closed their physical stores.

Netflix was the first company to stream movies and television shows, displacing virtually any other method of watching entertainment, including their own DVD movie rental business.

RICHARD PERRY/THE NEW YORK TIMES

An Uber black car in lower Manhattan.

It wasn't possible to join in mass games like Fortnite from your phone until the game developer Zynga pioneered mobile gaming in 2007. Zynga created an integrated social media gaming platform that didn't require a console or a PC to play. Instead, gamers could join using smartphones and tablets or through social networking sites such as Facebook.

WHAT'S NEXT?

Disruptive trends are emerging and developing in several areas of life.

The Sharing Economy. Through apps that allow private individuals to purchase rides or rent short-term lodging, Uber and Airbnb were early innovators in services that led to what is now called "the sharing economy." People can rent or sell underused assets — apartments, cars, bikes, clothing, freelance services — using online transactions, resulting in a dramatic change in the use of commercial services such as hotels and taxis, and posing a challenge for regulators.

Transportation. Under the leadership of Elon Musk, Tesla has spearheaded the design and production of electric cars, autonomous — self-driving — cars, and now rockets for private spaceflight. Musk also conceived of the hyperloop, a method of high-speed transportation using pods that travel through tubes, an idea the company Hyperloop One is developing.

Blockchain and Cryptocurrencies. Invented by Satoshi Nakamoto, blockchain technology is a digital ledger through which transactions of value — financial or otherwise — can be recorded. It was created to manage the cryptocurrency bitcoin, but innovators are starting to use blockchain technology in areas such as real estate and energy. Since bitcoin was introduced, several other cryptocurrencies have entered the market. Businesses have been slow to accept digital currency transactions, but investors have jumped in, generating interest and demand.

Editing Genes. Genetic engineers now know how to edit DNA using Crispr, a series of short repeating DNA sequences that bacteria use to identify specific viruses that attack them. This discovery has opened the door to many possible innovations, including treatments for conditions from cancer to sickle-cell anemia, correcting disease-causing mutations in humans, and modifying insects to prevent the spread of disease. It also raises ethical concerns — unregulated genetic engineering could result in eugenics, where parents select the traits they want in their children — and questions about how purposeful engineering of insects and plants will affect the environment.

Smart Homes and the Internet of Things. Innovative technology has shaped nearly every aspect of human life, and nowhere more than in the home. The Internet of Things was developed to seamlessly connect home life with the technology people use. From Amazon's voice-activated Echo and Google's Nest Learning Thermostat to internet-connected doorbells and security cameras, these technologies make life easier — but, as some people are starting to ask, do they make life better?

CHAPTER 1

The Sharing Economy

Now household names, Airbnb and Uber disrupted the traditional business-to-consumer paradigm by using technology to create peer-to-peer transactions. Individuals can now easily rent or sell assets they are not using — rooms, boats, rides and services — directly to each other through websites or apps. This paradigm shift has caused long-established consumer-based businesses to rethink some of their practices, while city and state governments seek ways to regulate sharing-economy businesses to ensure fair practices and tax revenue.

Europe Without Hotels

BY BENJI LANYADO | JULY 15, 2010

IN THE MIDDLE of a cool, cloudless Parisian afternoon, light was pouring into my guest room from a turn-of-the-century courtyard in the 10th Arrondissement. I clambered up to the loft bed, suspended above dark oak floors, and stared at the textiles shop sign swinging in the courtyard through the large, almost floor-to-ceiling windows.

A bottle of Bordeaux was breathing; other amenities included a pantry stocked with cereal, milk and yogurt. I also had a phone number to call if I needed dinner recommendations or, perhaps, extra shower gel. But I was happy sitting at the window, nodding at my new neighbors as they wheeled their bikes onto the street and headed into the cafe-lined Marais.

Hotel guests pay handsomely for such perks, but I wasn't in a hotel. Nor was I in some vacation rental. I was in the home of Julien Szeps, a 26-year-old chef whom I met through a new kind of short-term rental service called AirBnB.com. And the studio apartment was only 65 euros a night, about $80 at $1.23 to the euro. Not bad for an entire apartment with a full kitchen and bathroom, less than 10 minutes by foot from the Louvre.

While AirBnB is the largest of these new services, it isn't the only one. A half-dozen upstarts have emerged in the last two years — with names like iStopOver.com and Crashpadder.com — offering the convenience of a hotel, the comforts of a home and the price tag of an upmarket hostel. Call them social B&B networks, or maybe peer-to-peer hotels. Despite the confusing legal issues in many cities surrounding subletting, these new short-term rentals are making inroads into the hospitality industry, with hundreds of thousands of listings across the globe; there are over 3,500 short-term rentals in New York State alone.

Social networking first significantly influenced the world of travel in 1999 with the start of Couchsurfing, a service in which members offer a spare couch — or bed, or floor space — to fellow Couchsurfers, at no charge. It spawned a social phenomenon, and today counts almost two million people in 238 countries as members.

Social B&B networks are a natural next step, imposing an important distinction: money. The new sites appeal to a traveler's desire to see a city through local eyes (and from the vantage point of a resident's home), but add a hedge against disaster: with Couchsurfing you get what's given (it's free, after all), while sites like AirBnB generally provide detailed descriptions of the private rooms or apartments available for rent, along with protections if things go wrong.

In my own personal evolution, the proliferation of these new services couldn't have come at a better time. I used to Couchsurf frequently, from mattresses in Soviet-era tower blocks in Poland to luxurious condos in Madrid. But gradually, I've stopped using the service. These days I want a little privacy, especially if I'm traveling with my girlfriend. And I'm happy to pay a little money to guarantee a bed. Various vital signs are indicating that — sigh — I am growing up.

Unfortunately, my bank balance is still in the throes of adolescence, and upscale hotels are still well out of my reach. So I decided to test-drive a few of these new social B&Bs in a three-stop trip through Europe this spring. I began at home, in London. I decided to use Crashpadder.com, a two-year-old British-based site covering 59 countries, with a particularly strong selection of peer-to-peer listings in the city. You're lucky to get a London hotel for less than £100 (about $143) a night, but on the first page of my Crashpadder search results, I saw beds going for £21. In northern cities like Manchester or Leeds, there were beds for under £10.

To book one, I first had to create a short profile of myself. Unlike Expedia.com or other traditional hotel booking services, these sites rely on social networking, and everyone is encouraged to have a face and a little back story. I rewrote my entry three times before settling on: "Hello there. I am a 26-year-old from London. I like Chinese food and early '90s Italian football shirts."

Next, I scoured its listings. There was a luxury apartment in north London owned by an information technology professional who rents it out for £65 a night when he's out of town. In Bloomsbury, an American social worker had a room for £35 a night. But my dash across Europe necessitated a bed near St. Pancras International train station, so I opted for a "clean simple room with a chrome silver double bed" in the once-seedy district of Kings Cross for £50, owned by a 39-year-old vintage-clothing buyer.

Once you've found your room on Crashpadder, you can interact with the host through the internal messaging system and ask any questions you might have. (Do I need to bring towels? Do you have cats?) Hosts can ask for the money either up front or upon arrival.

A week after booking my room, I rolled my bag through the back streets of Kings Cross, aiming for a 1920s red-brick council building, where my host, Rachelle Hungerford-Boyle, lives on the third floor. It was the kind of unspectacular housing block that makes up vast swaths of the city, scattered in between the genteel stucco mansions that make it into the films.

I was buzzed through an electronic gate, and found Ms. Hungerford-Boyle hanging over the balcony, beckoning me up. I maneuvered my way through a soccer game among 8-year-olds and marched up to meet her. Inside her small apartment, the living room was dotted with extravagant secondhand dresses she had picked up in markets around the world. She'd sell her prize possession, a fluffy ball gown dangling from the window, only to Lady Gaga, she said.

My room, just over 10 by 10 feet, with a double bed and a door that locked, was good enough as a base. There was also a kitchen I was free to use, and a bathroom and shower. As this was my first social B&B experience, it was also immediately clear what I wasn't getting. I couldn't walk around naked, for example, and there wasn't a concierge who could make a dinner reservation for me. But there was Ms. Hungerford-Boyle, who, while making her temporary bed in the living room (where she sleeps when she has guests), told me how quickly the area was gentrifying, and suggested I visit Simmons, a trendy bar around the corner.

At Simmons later that evening, I thought about the £50 I had paid for Ms. Hungerford-Boyle's spare room. Founded in 2008, Crashpadder hasn't expanded as much as AirBnB (in early July it had listings in 898 cities compared with AirBnB's 5,378). I had a feeling that prices were somewhat scattershot, freed from the self-regulating bonds of a more mature marketplace. At my next stop, I wanted more.

The next morning I caught a Eurostar train to Paris, where my social B&B was booked through AirBnB.com. The site, which is based in San Francisco, was started by Joe Gebbia and Brian Chesky, roommates who decided to rent out their spare bedroom to people visiting the city for a design conference. An idea was born.

The site started operating in 2007, but it wasn't until the following year — during the Democratic and Republican conventions in Denver and St. Paul — that it started making waves. When Denver ran out of hotel beds, more than 300 residents used AirBnB to offer spare rooms. Unwittingly, they had opened a new tier in the holiday accommodation industry.

In Paris, AirBnB has places in every arrondissement, including \$13-a-night rooms in the western suburbs and \$285-a-night houseboats on the Seine. As the first Web site of its kind to grab the headlines, the system has already developed a large and loyal user base. Some properties have as many as 70 user-generated reviews, which give paying guests a greater sense of confidence. It is similar to how eBay works: you're more likely to buy from an eBay seller with good feedback.

My studio apartment there had received gushing write-ups from AirBnB users, including Francesca, who wrote that it was "peaceful, lovely and so cute!"

After paying \$97 for the booking via PayPal, the service sent me Mr. Szeps's e-mail and street addresses, and within an hour of arriving in Paris, I turned up in his courtyard, and entered his beautiful studio apartment.

Mr. Szeps joined AirBnB this year. "I used Craigslist when I wanted to rent the apartment before, but it was a little too risky. I didn't really know who was turning up," he said. "Then I used a normal B&B agency, but they made the apartment too expensive with their commission, and nobody came," he told me. Then he found AirBnB.

Since then, he has been a busy host, often receiving guests three nights a week. Some have stayed for as long as a month. By cutting out a traditional real estate agency, which can charge as much as 60 percent commission on top of a host's base rate, he can offer his apartment at a more competitive price. AirBnB tacks on 6 to 12 percent (the more expensive the rate, the smaller the commission). He even offers special deals during off-peak times. Though he didn't plan it, it has become a supplementary business for him.

As a restaurant professional, Mr. Szeps was also armed with tips, and he dispatched me to the Marché des Enfants Rouges, 10 minutes away in the northern Marais, where local traders have been selling fruits and vegetables since the 18th century. Today, West African and Asian stands are nestled between selections of Normandy cheese and produce from Île-de-France. For dinner, he recommended a Parisian classic: an al fresco picnic on the Canal St.-Martin, the splendid waterway that cuts an L-shaped swath through the northern part of the city center.

Not everyone is happy with these new social B&Bs. Innkeepers, for one, point out that they are unlicensed, uninsured and, depending on local real estate laws, against the law. In Paris, for example, renting a residential apartment for less than a year is considered illegal, though many pied-à-terre owners do it anyway. And in New York City, tenants and co-op owners are not usually allowed to sublet their apartments for short stays without permission from the landlord or co-op board. Still, neither apartment owners who stand to make money from these sites, nor the growing numbers of travelers looking for a middle ground between Couchsurfing and a traditional B&B or hotel are likely to be deterred.

When I contacted AirBnB about its stance on the questionable legality of listings in some cities, a spokesman declined to comment.

As for myself, I've stayed in many B&Bs in Paris on previous visits, and none were as comfortable as Mr. Szeps's apartment, or as good a value.

For the final stop, I caught an overnight train from the Gare Montparnasse to Barcelona, arriving on a beautifully clear Thursday morning. As I walked through the multistory 19th-century apartment blocks, I caught late-rising locals nursing coffees in corner cafes.

I was looking for an apartment I found through iStopOver, a year-old site based in Toronto that specializes in providing housing during large events like the World Cup and the Olympics, when visitor demand outstrips the supply of traditional hotels and B&Bs. The "Barcelona Penthouse" looked a little less homey, and more like a traditional vacation rental, than other listings, but I drooled over its outdoor terrace.

It was also in the Eixample neighborhood — a 15-minute walk from the tourist-drenched sidewalks of La Rambla, though it feels like a different city. There are no street performers or tacky stalls, just motorbikes parked outside apartment buildings with staggered roofs, and tier after tier of balconies overlooking quiet streets.

I buzzed an intercom two doors down from a tiny corner cafe, and was greeted by Arian Mostaedi, a 30-something publisher of coffee-table design books, who guided me through his modern one-bedroom apartment, with a glass kitchen table set for dinner for two, a sparkling bathroom with a glass shower stall, and a queen-size bed. And bingo — the large roof terrace with lounge chairs shrouded in citrus plants. For $105, it was a bargain.

Mr. Mostaedi bought the apartment with the intention of renting it out when he didn't have family staying — his mother is a regular guest. He, too, got frustrated with local agencies, and instead listed his apartment using a less expensive service in which he could vet guests, and interact with them before they arrived.

After the brief tour, I gave Mr. Mostaedi the code that allows him to collect my payment from iStopOver. That's one of the safeguards that iStopOver offers to guests. If a listing turns out to be fraudulent or misstated, you can refuse to give the owner the code, and the fee is refunded in full. Other services offer similar protections: AirBnB withholds a host's payment until 24 hours after guests check into an accommodation in order to fend off potential scammers, and Crashpadder uses credit card payments to verify guest identities (though it says it will monitor but not otherwise involve itself in any disputes).

IStopOver also offers to mediate in the event of a dispute, but I had no reason to try this out. The apartment was superb. So were Mr. Mostaedi's recommendations for restaurants and his hospitality. He left cookies and fruit in the apartment, and called me several times to check that everything was O.K. This is another perk of these new social B&B networks: hosts seem more inclined to take care of guests.

I spent most of my stay in Barcelona sprawled on my rooftop terrace, dipping in and out of the apartment for cold drinks and sliced fruit. I napped on a bed surrounded by exotic patterned pillows, with the balcony door open and the occasional whoosh of a car, or the sound of nattering shop owners, drifting up from the street. As the sun faded, a text arrived from Mr. Mostaedi, asking whether I was all right, and if I needed anything.

"All is good," I replied, as I watched my own private slice of Barcelona skyline turn from orange to red to blue.

The Smartphone Way to Beckon a Car

BY JOSHUA BRUSTEIN | MAY 16, 2011

HOW MUCH WOULD it be worth to use an app to call a car service, rather than hail a cab or call a black car?

Uber, a car service company based in San Francisco, is giving New Yorkers that option. As of May 4, its clever but costly system has been available in New York.

Once you sign up for Uber's free app and enter your credit card information, you can call a car by opening the app and telling it your location. The system tells you how long the driver will take to arrive, and a map will show the car's progress as it makes its way to you.

The vehicles are particularly nice by livery standards; you do feel important when a black Cadillac Escalade pulls up to your stoop. There is also a feeling of camaraderie with the drivers, who act as though everyone in the car is in on a secret. The fare (tip included) is automatically charged to your credit card upon arriving at your destination, and you receive a receipt by e-mail.

Of course, the gee-whiz factor comes with a price: The base rate is $7, with an additional $3.90 charged each mile, or $0.95 a minute. A ride that would have cost about $20 in a yellow cab costs $36 with Uber. The premium seems steep, considering that the service being offered is basically the same one you would get with a black car.

In fact, when I used Uber to summon a ride from Astoria, Queens, the driver took about 20 minutes to arrive, much longer than the 5 or 10 minutes I usually have to wait if I call a local livery service. Still, in Manhattan, the fastest way to catch a ride is usually to step off the curb and stick a hand in the air.

Several companies are pursuing even more ambitious car-service projects, in which riders would use their phones to find people nearby who are headed the same way, and then share the car — and the bill.

But these companies are hobbled by a lack of critical mass. Weeels, which has the most developed app, claims 4,500 registered users, not nearly enough to be able to count on reliably finding shares. I spent a weekend looking to share rides from Brooklyn, Manhattan and Queens at different times, and never managed to do so.

The app allows users to call for solo rides as well, but the service is not as good as Uber's — once, when I used it, the car simply failed to arrive — and the cost is comparable. Developing a ride-sharing system is no easy task — even the city's Taxi and Limousine Commission scaled back its cab-sharing experiment in recent months. Uber declined to say whether it would try to start its own.

Companies Built on Sharing Balk When It Comes to Regulators

BY DAVID STREITFELD | APRIL 21, 2014

IN THE NEWFANGLED sharing economy, questions about safety, taxes and regulation have tended to be an afterthought. That has helped propel companies like Uber, Airbnb and Lyft into the stratosphere.

But regulators as well as some elected officials across the country are increasingly questioning the presumptions and tactics of these start-ups, especially the notion that laws do not apply to them.

The companies are fighting back by rallying their impassioned and growing customer base. And they are stocking up on lawyers and lobbyists.

The latest confrontation comes Tuesday as Airbnb, the largest housing rental company, goes to court in Albany. It is fighting an effort by New York regulators to collect the names of Airbnb hosts who are breaking the law by renting out multiple properties for short periods.

Airbnb, which is now estimated to be worth $10 billion, is framing the dispute as a case of government scooping up more data than it needs for purposes that are vague.

"He claims to be targeting a small number of bad actors," said David Hantman, Airbnb's head of global public policy, referring to the New York attorney general, Eric T. Schneiderman. "But he is asking for data on thousands of regular New Yorkers."

In a blog post, Airbnb said the regulators' plan was to accuse Airbnb hosts in court "of being bad neighbors and bad citizens." It added: "They'll call us slumlords and tax cheats. They might even say we all faked the moon landing."

It is against the law in New York City to rent out an apartment for less than a month, a 2010 measure meant to curb unregulated hotels. Mr. Schneiderman says 60 percent of Airbnb rentals in New York are illegal.

Existing laws, Airbnb executives say, do not fit the sharing economy.

"There are laws for people and there are laws for business, but you are a new category, a third category, people as businesses," Brian Chesky, Airbnb's chief executive, told an audience last fall. "As hosts, you are microentrepreneurs, and there are no laws written for microentrepreneurs."

Micah Lasher, Mr. Schneiderman's chief of staff, fired back that "being innovative is not a defense to breaking the law."

Calling consumers to arms is a defense that has worked well for the businesses of the sharing economy. Last week, ride-sharing companies collected enough signatures in Seattle to overturn a new City Council measure that limited their growth. This week, they are trying to fight an effort by Arizona legislators to introduce some modest controls on their business.

Attempts at old-fashioned regulation are being cheered on by the taxi and hotel industries, who feel their livelihood is being threatened. Affordable-housing advocates are now joining the fray, saying companies like Airbnb are worsening a crisis.

"You are throwing gasoline on a fire that the rest of us are trying to put out," a coalition of housing groups, Real Affordability for All, asserted Monday in an open letter to Airbnb.

Until recently, start-ups generally avoided areas that were heavily regulated, like transporting people and renting rooms. Even a well-funded start-up did not have the money, time or patience to wrestle approval from bureaucrats.

Then, a few years ago, Silicon Valley had a collective insight: Better to ask forgiveness than permission.

At a recent valley conference on the sharing economy, Kevin Laws of AngelList, a site that unites start-ups and investors, explained that "the approach almost all start-ups take is to see if they can be successful fast enough so they can have enough money to work with the regulators."

Many start-ups define "working with" regulators as simply accusing them of holding back innovation. But Mr. Laws said regulators were trying to balance many competing interests. "This assumption that they're always bad in my experience has been almost 100 percent wrong," he said.

The New York regulators are seeking through a subpoena the names of landlords they think are breaking the law.

On Jan. 31, there were 19,522 listings for New York City properties on Airbnb from 15,677 hosts, according to data the attorney general submitted to the court. But nearly a third of the listings were from only 12 percent of the hosts.

One Airbnb landlord had 127 listings in Manhattan on a single weekend last fall. Sixteen other landlords had at least 15 listings each.

Even as Airbnb was increasing the volume of its attack on regulators on Monday, it was deleting numerous New York hosts from its site.

"When we examined our community in New York, we found that some property managers weren't providing a quality, local experience to guests," the company said in a blog post. The removed landlords controlled a total of 2,000 rooms.

The regulators took Airbnb's action as proof that people are indeed abusing the site, and that Airbnb knows it.

"The publicly available data suggests that a disproportionate share of Airbnb's business comes not from struggling artists and grandmothers but rather large commercial enterprises," said Mr. Lasher, the chief of staff. He added that the "string of attacks" on the attorney general was "a transparent effort to distract from our investigation."

On Tuesday morning, Airbnb intends to put forth a fresh attack on Mr. Schneiderman, releasing a memo that plays up those struggling small stakeholders.

"Kimberly is an Airbnb host on the Lower East Side," the memo says. "She has a chronic illness that prevents her from working." Kimberly is quoted directly: "My husband and I spent countless nights wondering if and when we would lose our home, or if we would have to stop treatment to keep a roof over our heads." She concludes, "Airbnb saved us."

What both sides seem to agree on is that being a New York landlord on Airbnb can be lucrative.

Two years ago, Airbnb hosts in New York were making an average of $21,000 a year, the company said at the time, and some as much as $100,000.

Of the top forty highest-grossing Airbnb hosts in New York, each took in at least $400,000 over the last three years, Mr. Schneiderman said. Collectively, they have grossed more than $35 million over the last three years.

Businesses Turn to Airbnb

BY MATT KRUPNICK | OCT. 6, 2014

LAUREN HAUBER has moved past the days of trudging down the hotel corridor with an ice bucket.

Like a growing number of business travelers, Ms. Hauber, a San Francisco resident, and her co-workers have started staying in apartments and houses managed through Airbnb, which in July started a site aimed at attracting more business travelers. The service allows travelers — business and leisure — to rent space for short periods.

Ms. Hauber and two colleagues rented a three-bedroom condominium in downtown Austin, Tex., for this week's SXSW Eco conference. The apartment was less expensive and more convenient than hotels in the area, she said, and it had other benefits.

"I really like having a kitchen," said Ms. Hauber, who does business development for Wildlife Works, an environmental firm in Mill Valley, Calif. "A lot of times they'll have washers and dryers. I don't feel like I'm losing anything by using an Airbnb."

Companies large and small, increasingly focused on budgets, are starting to look beyond hotels to apartments and houses.

"We're seeing really kind of shocking growth in the use of Airbnb by business travelers," said Tim MacDonald, an executive vice president with Concur, which designs software for managing business expenses and travel. Use of Airbnb properties by companies using the Concur system has surged in the past year, Mr. MacDonald said. San Francisco, New York and Austin, as well as Paris and London, have been particularly popular destinations for business travelers opting for Airbnb, he said.

The service has been embraced especially in San Francisco, where hotel occupancy rates hover around 90 percent, said Joe D'Alessandro, president and chief executive of the San Francisco Travel Association.

During technology conferences like Oracle OpenWorld and Macworld, "the city's basically in sellout mode," Mr. D'Alessandro said. Before Airbnb, he added, "there were times when the city was full and people just couldn't get in."

The trend is part of a growing reliance on the so-called sharing economy, which also includes companies like the Uber car service and TaskRabbit, where clients can find people to help with everyday chores and other tasks.

Although Airbnb declined to give the number of business travelers using the service, at least 55 companies are using the site to plan business trips, said Lex Bayer, who heads Airbnb's business development. The site's new business portal mostly excludes shared apartments and quirkier properties, like boats and tree houses, in favor of entire houses or apartments, Mr. Bayer said.

The service has proved popular with property owners, he said, especially since business travel helps fill vacant sites during the week.

"Typically business travelers are good travelers," he said. "Hosts enjoy having them."

Among the hosts who have benefited is Steve Puryear, who said up to two-thirds of the guests in his Austin condominium — including Ms. Hauber and her colleagues — were business travelers. The headline on his Airbnb listing makes his preference clear: "Perfect 4 Executives/ Professionals."

"I was getting a lot of bachelor parties and stuff," he said. "I wanted to steer toward business travelers. There are long-term residents in the building and noise complaints are expensive."

Airbnb's primary competitor, HomeAway, has not focused on business travel and has no plans to do so, said Jon Gray, its senior vice president for the Americas. Business trips account for 2 percent of the company's bookings, he said.

HomeAway, which runs VRBO and VacationRentals.com, among other sites, is looking at a new site focusing on homes in urban areas, however, Mr. Gray said. Increased business travel may "come along for the ride," he said.

Increased competition from Airbnb and others will force hotels to find ways to bring back business travelers, said Michael W. McCormick, executive director and chief operating officer of the Global Business Travel Association. For now, he said, it is no wonder that companies are using the new service.

"Travelers and companies are always looking for creative options," Mr. McCormick said. "From that perspective, everybody's intrigued."

Like Uber, which has run afoul of taxi operators and transit regulators around the world, Airbnb has battled hotel owners and officials in cities from San Francisco to New York, as well as in Europe, as governments try to figure out how to tax and regulate the sharing economy.

But businesses have started to embrace Airbnb in the meantime. The service has come in handy for GitHub, a San Francisco-based software start-up with about 150 employees who work outside the Bay Area. Without Airbnb, many of those employees would have trouble finding hotel rooms during conferences, said Brian Doll, a GitHub vice president.

"All the hotels are pretty much booked," he said. "Anything that's left is going to be six times the market rate."

Airbnb properties, which often include common areas like family or dining rooms, also give employees more working space than a hotel room, Mr. Doll said. "We might have four to six people traveling to a location to do work together," he said. "Hotel rooms aren't well suited for that."

The business travel market is still big enough for both hotels and Airbnb, said Mr. McCormick of the Global Business Travel Association. Many travelers will opt for the convenience of room service over the freedom of a kitchen, he said.

"Yes, they are all competing," he said. "But I think Airbnb is bringing something different to a different segment of the marketplace."

In an Uber World, Fortune Favors the Freelancer

OPINION | BY TYLER COWEN | JUNE 27, 2015

WITH THE RISE of companies like Uber, entrepreneurs in a variety of fields are extending the concept of connecting customers and workers in what is sometimes called the new sharing economy. There are now online services for private tutors, dog walkers and delivery of packages and groceries, among numerous other options, and it is likely that these ventures will expand.

Many taxi drivers dislike the competition from Uber, but we need to think more systematically about the winners and losers as these new institutions develop. The greater convenience they provide consumers is obvious, but is this generally a good or bad thing for people on the other side of the market, the workers? One recent study, by Jonathan V. Hall of Uber and Alan B. Krueger, a professor of economics at Princeton, supported by Uber, suggested that Uber drivers earned more than typical taxi drivers and chauffeurs. A study of Airbnb by the economist Gene Sperling, in conjunction with Airbnb, found that the service helped supplement middle-class incomes.

Recently the California Labor Commissioner's Office ruled that one Uber driver was an employee rather than an independent contractor. Uber is appealing the ruling, and it has prevailed in some other states. We don't yet know how the laws surrounding these services will develop, but the economic efficiencies of institutions like Uber and Airbnb appear to be robust.

Such services are likely to continue to spread. If they do, what else is there to say about their broader implications? In the absence of a lot of systematic data, how might economists think through the effects of these new developments?

On the positive side, the so-called sharing economy allows workers to use their time more flexibly. Drivers can earn money without working full time, and without having to wait around at taxi stands for the next passenger. The workers can use their newly acquired spare time for other purposes, including studying for college, teaching themselves programming or simultaneously offering themselves out for different sharing services: If no one wants a ride, go help someone with repairs around the house.

In short, these developments benefit those workers who are willing and able to turn their spare time to productive uses. These workers tend to be self-starters and people who are good at shifting roles quickly. Think of them as disciplined and ambitious task switchers. That describes a lot of people, but of course, it isn't everybody.

That's where some of the problems come in. Uber drivers are much more likely to have a college degree than are taxi drivers or chauffeurs, according to the Hall and Krueger study. It found striking differences between the two groups: 48 percent of Uber drivers have a college degree or higher, whereas that figure is only 18 percent for taxi drivers and chauffeurs.

Only some workers benefit when each hour, or each 15-minute gap, is up for sale. One way to put the general principle is this: The more efficient market technologies become, the more important are human capabilities and backgrounds in determining who prospers and who does not.

To get a better handle on how some workers might lose, consider a hypothetical situation in which such services — and all freelancing and outsourcing services — do not exist. Let's say a software company receives periodic contracts to execute projects, but it has to rely entirely on current full-time staff. The company then must train its workers to handle a wide variety of possible projects, and so the amount and cost of corporate in-house education go up. But all things being equal, because this training costs something to the company, worker wages will be lower.

In this case, those workers who benefit will be those who need that push from the in-house education to acquire new knowledge. But some self-starting workers might have learned the material on their own anyway. Those workers receive more in-house education than they need, which, in turn, means they are paid lower wages and might well be worse off than they would have been in an economy that encourages self-training and freelance opportunities. One implication is that if the Uber idea spreads, it could discourage corporate training and may require that workers have stronger educational backgrounds. Ideally, formal education should refocus to prepare people for subsequent self-instruction and retraining.

Workers are likely to be evaluated in different ways, too. The Uber driver, who can be rated by customers on the web after a ride, without face-to-face interaction, has a stronger incentive to be nicer, and to offer a clean vehicle and bottles of water, compared with a traditional cabdriver.

At the moment, one problem with many online ratings is that the information isn't all publicly useful; for instance, a good Uber rating remains within Uber and cannot easily be exported to market a driver for other jobs or opportunities. Perhaps in the future workers might have the option of being certified by Uber or other services in a more general and publicly verifiable manner. That could make such services useful for upward mobility, and it might make their credentials competitive with those of some lower-tier colleges and universities.

Even if we don't know how important all of the new services will be, it's already clear that many consumers like them. It's also evident that at least some workers can benefit from the new arrangements, although the effect on the less educated workers seems to be an important issue.

Still, we shouldn't be trying to turn back the clock, but rather figuring out how to make the best of this fascinating but sometimes unsettling new world. We are just getting started.

TYLER COWEN IS A PROFESSOR OF ECONOMICS AT GEORGE MASON UNIVERSITY.

What Uber Can Learn From Airbnb's Global Expansion

BY MARK SCOTT | JULY 7, 2015

LAST WEEK, the home-sharing service Airbnb had more than 40,000 listings in Paris, making the French capital the company's most popular destination for travelers looking to rent a room or an entire apartment. Paris officials applaud it for bringing innovation to the city's hotel industry.

The ride-hailing company Uber had a much more difficult week.

Thousands of Parisian taxi drivers took to the streets to protest UberPop, the company's low-cost service that's similar to UberX in the United States. French politicians denounced the company for defying the country's transport laws. And two of Uber's top executives in France were detained by the police and accused of operating an illegal taxi business. By Friday, the company had suspended UberPop across the country.

Uber and Airbnb are similar in many ways. Both born in San Francisco, the companies are now two of the largest entrants in the so-called on-demand economy, in which services are available at the touch of a smartphone button. They are both flush with investor money — with valuations in the tens of billions of dollars — and are using the cash to expand rapidly around the world.

But the starkly different paths in France for these companies lay bare contrasting strategies as they encounter the world of global regulators. Since it began in 2009, Uber has entered city after city, in Europe and elsewhere, with a largely catch-me-if-you-can attitude. Airbnb, which offers more rooms than traditional hotel groups like Hilton and InterContinental, has instead tilted toward courting local politicians in many of its most popular markets.

So far, Uber's approach has not significantly slowed it down. The company operates in more than 300 cities in almost 60 countries and is valued by investors at more than $40 billion. But Uber's aggressive attitude has put it at odds with regulators in many of the cities that are crucial to the company's global ambitions.

"A lot of these start-ups initially don't think much about regulation," said Thilo Koslowski, head of the automotive practice at Gartner, a technology research company in California. "It's all about having a punch strategy. They do things first, then ask questions later. As they mature, that starts to change."

Airbnb has not gone unscathed by regulators. It has faced significant clampdowns in American cities like New York, where some local policy makers have argued that Airbnb rentals could reduce the amount of long-term housing in the city. And last year, Airbnb was fined in Europe for the first time for violating a law in the Catalonia region of Spain that forbids renting individual rooms for tourism purposes. Airbnb is appealing the roughly $33,000 fine.

But by and large, Airbnb's approach has been to work with regulators, not against them.

In France, local Airbnb rentals started popping up a few months after the company was founded in 2008. Initially, the start-up had limited contact with local regulators, finding few who understood its business. But by 2012, shortly after the Paris listings began growing quickly, Airbnb opened an office in the city and started speaking regularly with local authorities. They continued to do so in 2013, when new housing legislation was being debated.

Now, to clamp down on illegal vacation rentals, a team of investigators in Paris regularly conducts inspections, with fines of up to $28,000 for people who break the law, a rule that Airbnb supports. In addition, by early 2016, the company will start collecting a tourist tax from its users on behalf of Paris authorities, making the French capital the second city in Europe after Amsterdam to offer that service.

This approach with regulators is "about finding partners within governments that understand the sharing economy," said Patrick Robinson, head of public policy in Europe for Airbnb. "We want to explain what is happening out there because at some point, they will want to regulate this."

Uber began operating in France in late 2011, and the company says it initially found it difficult to set up meetings with French officials. Two years later, lawmakers were trying to put limits on the service, proposing new rules that would force any ride-booking service like Uber to wait at least 15 minutes before drivers could pick up new passengers, giving traditional taxi drivers a head start.

Last year, executives from the company began holding increasingly regular meetings with French lawmakers, part of a larger effort by the company to better engage regulators. By then, though, the pressure that had been applied by well-connected taxi groups had mostly won in France.

A new transport law, which went into force this year, requires all chauffeurs to have a professional license and restricts drivers from using geolocation software to show the whereabouts of their cars, rules that essentially prevent UberPop drivers from working legally. Authorities in Germany, Spain and the Netherlands also have banned Uber's low-cost offering, saying it amounts to unfair competition for traditional taxis.

Uber continued to operate UberPop in France, arguing in local courts that the transport law is unconstitutional. French police officers, however, have started issuing fines to some UberPop drivers, and the company's offices were raided in March during investigations that remain open. In response to the latest protests, Uber suspended its low-cost service on Friday.

"We're providing an additional option for moving around cities," Antoine Aubert, a director of public policy at Uber, told European politicians last week. "We're facing restrictions with outdated regulation in countries like France, Spain and Germany."

A company spokesman declined to comment further on its dealings with regulators.

Uber's problems escalated last week, when taxi drivers blocked roads, burned tires and attacked drivers who they thought were working for Uber. Two of the company's senior executives in France also were detained and will stand trial in September on charges including "deceptive commercial practices" and illegally organizing taxi services through Uber's low-cost service.

"Modernity is innovation, the quality of service, the sharing economy," said Bernard Cazeneuve, France's interior minister, after the anti-Uber demonstrations spread across the country. "It is not black-market jobs and clandestine work organized against the rule of law by Uber."

In recent months, Uber has appeared more willing to engage with lawmakers. At a conference in January attended by many European officials in Munich, Travis Kalanick, the company's chief executive, said Uber wanted to find ways to operate within the law across the 28-member European Union. By allowing Uber to operate, Mr. Kalanick argued, the company could create up to 50,000 new jobs for drivers.

But as recent events in France have shown, the company sometimes remains willing to push ahead regardless of the opinions of lawmakers.

"Any government can shut you down, so you have to be willing to play the regulatory game," said Gerald R. Faulhaber, professor emeritus of business economics and public policy at the Wharton School at the University of Pennsylvania. "You need to work with regulators. There's no way around that."

AURELIEN BREEDEN CONTRIBUTED REPORTING.

Airbnb and Uber Mobilize Vast User Base to Sway Policy

BY CONOR DOUGHERTY AND MIKE ISAAC | NOV. 4, 2015

SAN FRANCISCO — Over the last few years, so-called sharing companies like Airbnb and Uber — online platforms that allow strangers to pay one another for a room or a ride — have established footholds in thousands of communities well before local regulators have figured out how to deal with them.

Now, as cities grapple with the growth of these services and try to pass rules for how they should operate, the companies are fighting back by turning their users into a vast political operation that can be mobilized at any sign of a threat.

Airbnb offered the latest and most vociferous example of this on Wednesday. Fresh off defeating a San Francisco measure that would have severely curtailed the company's business in its hometown, Airbnb staged a news conference that functioned as a warning shot to other cities thinking about proposing new regulations.

The event was billed as a debriefing to discuss the defeat of Proposition F, which would have toughened existing rules for the service by, among other things, cutting the number of nights people could rent out rooms in their homes.

But the briefing was less about the actual election than an attempt to turn the results into a mandate for the sharing economy.

Chris Lehane, a Washington political operative who now serves as Airbnb's head of global policy and public affairs, framed Proposition F as a hotel-industry-led attack on the middle class.

In this city of about 840,000 people, roughly $8 million was raised by groups opposed to Proposition F — about eight times the amount raised by the proposition's backers, according to records filed with the San Francisco Ethics Commission.

JIM WILSON/THE NEW YORK TIMES

Chris Lehane, Airbnb's head of global policy and public affairs, talking about the company's successful opposition to San Francisco's Proposition F in 2015.

Much of that money was spent mobilizing Airbnb hosts and users, Mr. Lehane said. Still, he repeatedly homed in on one of the company's most important talking points: Airbnb's victory was a win for the middle class.

"Cities recognize where the world is going, right, they understand that you're either going to go forward or you're going to go backward," he said. "They understand that in a time of economic inequality, this is a question of whose side are you on: Do you want to be on the side of the middle class, or do you want to be opposed to the middle class?"

Airbnb is preparing for more fights. Mr. Lehane said the company was working to organize voting blocs in other cities where it operates. By the end of next year, he said, the company has a goal of creating 100 "clubs" made up of Airbnb home-sharers — sort of like local unions.

Companies like Airbnb and Uber have become multibillion-dollar companies by employing a kind of guerrilla growth strategy in which they set up a modest team of workers in a city and immediately start providing their services to the public, whether local laws allow them to or not.

Uber, the ride-hailing behemoth now valued at more than $50 billion, operates in more than 300 cities around the world. Airbnb is available in 34,000 cities, and more than 60 million people have used the service. Investors value the company at $24 billion — higher than the hotel giant Marriott International's valuation.

Those billions are predicated on lots of future growth. So both companies have hired seasoned political operatives to woo legislators and beat back regulatory threats.

Mr. Lehane, a former political operative in the Clinton administration, was nicknamed the Master of Disaster for his no-holds-barred approach to winning political fights. David Plouffe, a former adviser to President Obama, is now a senior adviser to Uber and a member of its board.

Mr. Lehane and Mr. Plouffe have both tried to frame their companies as middle-class saviors in a moment of economic anxiety and income inequality — themes that are playing out in the presidential election as well. Jeb Bush and other Republicans have bragged about their Uber rides on the campaign trail, praising these companies as the future of self-sufficient employment.

Democrats have taken a more cautious approach. Hillary Rodham Clinton has repeatedly questioned what such employment means for workers' rights. Liberal economists who advise Mrs. Clinton have criticized such part-time labor as yet another means to chip away at workers' benefits.

But such companies have a potent tool in the form of their platforms and smartphone apps, and they have shown little hesitation in using it to encourage their users to protest or vote.

In New York, Mayor Bill de Blasio backed a proposal this year that would cap the number of Uber drivers on the road in Manhattan. Uber fought back by tweaking its smartphone app with a special "de Blasio" feature to show users in New York how hard it would be to get an Uber ride under those caps.

"This is what Uber will look like in NYC if Mayor de Blasio's Uber cap bill passes," the app said.

In the news conference on Wednesday, Mr. Lehane used a slide show to portray people who rent their property on Airbnb as a potent voting bloc that, like the members of a labor union, will reliably show up to vote, even in low-turnout elections like Tuesday's.

"There is going to be more people doing home-sharing tomorrow than there are today, there is going to be more the day after that," he said. "This is now a movement."

Movement or not, some have already tried to curb these companies' growing political power. One of the other measures in Tuesday's election was Proposition C, a complicated proposal that would, among other things, make companies like Airbnb disclose any money they use to encourage hosts to show up at city meetings.

And it is unlikely the Airbnb debate in San Francisco has ended with the election.

On Tuesday, San Franciscans also elected Aaron Peskin, a longtime San Francisco progressive, to its Board of Supervisors. In an interview, Mr. Peskin promised the Airbnb issue would not go away.

"I think Airbnb would be well served to negotiate a workable, enforceable compromise" to curb "the most egregious excesses that result in the loss of permanent, affordable rental housing stock," he said. "Or this is likely to be a perennial issue at the ballot."

AMY CHOZICK CONTRIBUTED REPORTING FROM NEW YORK.

Airbnb Pledges to Work with Cities and Pay 'Fair Share' of Taxes

BY MIKE ISAAC | NOV. 11, 2015

SAN FRANCISCO — A week ago, Airbnb fired off a warning shot to cities that it would fight back if municipal officials proposed rules that might curtail its home-sharing service.

"There is going to be more people doing home-sharing tomorrow than there are today; there is going to be more the day after that," Chris Lehane, Airbnb's head of global policy and public affairs, said at the time to underline how the company is unstoppable. "This is now a movement."

This week, Airbnb dialed back its rhetoric.

The start-up, which is based in San Francisco, on Wednesday introduced a lengthy treatise pledging a renewed spirit of cooperation with local governments. Called the Airbnb Community Compact, the document outlines several ways that the popular company plans to work with municipalities, including sharing anonymized data on the hosts and guests who use the service, preventing illegal hotel landlords from operating on the platform, and promising to pay its "fair share" of hotel and tourist taxes in cities that have them.

"Given the size of the Airbnb community, this just seems like the right time for us to be very specific about the types of commitments we're willing to make," Mr. Lehane said in an interview. "Cities are looking to do the right thing, and they need the right information to do so."

The shifts in Airbnb's messaging show the tightrope the company is walking as it tries to expand its business in a tricky regulatory environment. Many towns do not have rules in place to deal with an online service for people to rent out their rooms or homes on a short-term basis. The company, which is now seven years old, has not waited for permission to operate in many locales. In some cases, Airbnb has avoided city-mandated hotel taxes or strict safety regulations that apply to hotels and regulated bed-and-breakfasts.

JASON HENRY FOR THE NEW YORK TIMES

A sign in the window of a convenience store on Market Street supporting Prop F in San Francisco, Calif.

Airbnb has had plenty of momentum, now with upward of two million listings across more than 34,000 cities, and with private investors valuing the company at more than $24 billion. That has allowed Airbnb to flex some of its muscles with local regulators — but too much flexing can backfire.

Airbnb found this out recently after dueling in the run-up to a San Francisco election over a ballot initiative that would have cut the supply of short-term rentals, affecting the company's business in its hometown. Airbnb spent more than $8 million fighting the measure, called Proposition F, and the company came under intense criticism for its series of anti-Prop F billboards and ads in the city.

Airbnb worked to help defeat Prop F, but then held a news conference in which the company said it could mobilize its users to vote down proposed rules that were aimed against it in other cities. The language was not well received by some policy makers, including Aaron Peskin, who was elected to San Francisco's Board of Supervisors last week. He said at the time that the Airbnb issue would not go away.

"If Airbnb is not at least somewhat flexible on their part, cities will just dig in their heels," said Rob Atkinson, president of the Information Technology and Innovation Foundation, referring to the company's changing tone with municipalities.

Many of Airbnb's messaging changes lately originated with Mr. Lehane, who, after performing consulting work for the company for years, officially joined Airbnb full-time in August. Mr. Lehane, a longtime political operative, brings to the job a reputation for hands-on, bare-knuckle sparring with Washington insiders.

Mr. Lehane said Airbnb's messages were not inconsistent. The mobilization of voters was meant to fight against the hotel industry, which has not been receptive to home sharing, he said.

"We have always said we want to partner with cities," Mr. Lehane said. "As Prop F in San Francisco made clear, our community will fight and win if the hotel interests are threatening the economic lifeline of home sharing, but on the natural we would prefer to be lovers of cities and not fighting with the hotel industry."

The pledges within the Airbnb Community Compact are intended to give local governments data and other information that they have been asking for from the start-up. Some municipalities have long appealed for Airbnb data to help them crack down on illegal operators of large blocks of rooms, for instance.

That issue was front and center last year in New York City. Last May, after a protracted battle in court, Airbnb agreed to hand over anonymized data on the company's hosts in the city to Eric T. Schneiderman, the New York State attorney general. The goal, Mr. Schneiderman said at the time, was to hunt down so-called illegal hotels using the service.

On Wednesday, Mr. Schneiderman said Airbnb's Community Compact "is a transparent ploy by Airbnb to act like a good corporate citizen when it is anything but. The company has all of the information and tools it needs to clean up its act. Until it does, no one should take this press release seriously."

Airbnb has also faced regulatory issues internationally, in cities including Barcelona and Berlin.

Taking a cooperative stance with cities may not only help Airbnb on the regulation front but may also ease any concerns by hosts who rent out rooms and homes on the service. On Thursday, the company plans an event in Paris for hosts, where the company said it would share tips to help them make more money. The gathering will also serve both as an incentive for hosts to keep using Airbnb and as a strategy to help cut down on the churn of people listing homes for rent once or twice without returning.

Other on-demand companies have also had to soften their approaches with local governments. Uber, the ride-hailing giant valued at more than $50 billion, was known for its hard-charging stance into cities, bypassing local legislators until it reached a tipping point with consumers.

But David Plouffe, the former adviser to President Obama who is now Uber's senior policy adviser and a company board member, has courted regulators with appeals about how the service can help lift stagnant wages and rejuvenate the middle class.

"All of these companies have organized to deal with this risk to reputation," said Derek van Bever, the director of the Forum for Growth and Innovation at Harvard Business School. "The regulatory risk warning light is flashing bright red on their management dashboards."

What the Sharing Economy Really Delivers: Entitlement

BY GINIA BELLAFANTE | JAN. 26, 2018

NOT LONG AGO a friend told me how she had come to end her relationship with WeWork, the entrepreneurial-class fun house that at recent count had been rolled out in 59 cities around the world. A playwright and producer, she had been renting office space at a WeWork location in Brooklyn when one night a little over a year ago, she showed up after a rehearsal to get some rewriting done and found a party in progress.

As she settled down at her desk, she could see that across the hall a couple was getting down to business of the kind that did not involve calculating price-earnings ratios. Things were loud and many people around her, none of whom she knew, were drunk, but she was determined to spend the next hour or so accomplishing something despite the ambient hedonism.

That effort was thwarted when two men who comfortably fit the stereotype of young hustlers on Planet Start-Up approached her desk, sat on it and began a vaguely menacing flirtation — poking at her computer, reading what was on the screen, poking at her. The next day she decided to render a complaint about the bacchanal she had encountered — if that were what she wanted, she could save $1,000 a month and set up a laptop on a curb in the meatpacking district on a Friday at midnight.

But where or to whom would one deliver a grievance? WeWork makes it easier to speak with a human being than other innovators born of the Silicon Valley ethos that talking on the phone is as crude an anachronism as cleaning your girdle with a washboard, but it is still not a simple matter. When my friend finally reached someone at the company, she was greeted solicitously and told she could have a desk on another part of the floor away from the offending fraternity. But moving a woman around to accommodate male misbehavior felt like a solution Roger Sterling would have come up with during the

HILARY SWIFT FOR THE NEW YORK TIMES

The Wing in SoHo is a woman-only co-working space, designed to offer a refuge from the air-hockey culture of places like WeWork.

second season of "Mad Men." Disillusioned, she left and sought another arrangement.

The co-working revolution has offered as one of its lures the blurred distinction between work life and private life, but it is precisely the obscuring of those boundaries — in Hollywood, in the restaurant industry, in theater and so on — that created the opportunities for harassment and abuse over and over again in the first place: the meetings called in hotel rooms, the research projects conducted at country houses, the bathrobes as uniforms.

WeWork's website features a page entitled "What Is WeWork's Beer Keg Policy?" an idea that presumably has no analog at Proctor & Gamble. The policy, in fact, allows for kegs to be open on weekdays until approximately 9:30 p.m., but insists that they close on weekends "as they are intended to be a workplace amenity."

As people become their own brands, in the nonsense argot of the new economy, as work increasingly happens anywhere and everywhere, disaggregated from institutions and hierarchies and protocols that can offer various protections and clear channels of recourse, the policing of harassment will face new challenges. Already many women have chosen to bypass the air-hockey subculture of conventional co-working facilities for all-female alternatives like The Wing in New York or Rise Collaborative in St. Louis. They are tired of men and their predations and inefficiencies.

In so many ways the virtue capitalists who have built the sharing economy on the premise that they are making the world a more just and equitable place, as they generate billions of dollars for themselves, have simply delivered more of the status quo. A report, soon to be released from McGill University's School of Urban Planning, shows just who is and who is not benefiting from the income streams produced by Airbnb.

Titled "The High Cost of Short-Term Rentals in New York City," the study is one of several that have examined the impact of Airbnb on affordable housing in various cities over the years. Looking at data covering the period from September 2014 to August of last year, it highlights just how unevenly revenue is distributed among hosts in New York City. Last year the top 10 percent of hosts earned 48 percent of all revenue. This amounted to $318 million. The bottom 80 percent earned just 32 percent, or $209 million.

In response, Christopher Nulty, the head of public affairs for Airbnb, said that the study's methodology was faulty, that the authors maintained "an anti-home-sharing bias" (the study was paid for by the hotel industry), and that the company supports legislation that would restrict home sharing by landlords to a single home. The study lands at a moment, though, when a Chelsea landlord has just been hit with a lawsuit by the city for turning a four-story walk-up building into an illegal hotel, using Airbnb, and taking rent-stablized apartments away from tenants.

And in New York, as the debate about congestion pricing has intensified, it has become very clear that the proliferation of ride-hailing apps has, in fact, caused a great deal more traffic. Midtown speeds have slowed to an average of 4.7 miles an hour from 6.5 miles per hour five years ago. There are now 103,000 for-hire cars operating in the city, and a report issued late last year found that cars operating as part of ride-hailing services average 11 minutes of unoccupied time between dropping one passenger off and picking up another. The comparable time for yellow taxis is eight minutes. Think about that the next time you want to Uber your way to that no-cash fast-food place with locally grown and sustainable everything.

The Whatchamacallit Economy

BY STEVEN GREENHOUSE | DEC. 16, 2016

IT'S A HIP, fast-growing sector of the economy, filled with headline-grabbing companies: Uber, Lyft, Airbnb, Task Rabbit. But there's a gnawing problem: People aren't sure what to call it. Many critics dislike the term most commonly used, the "sharing economy," because there often isn't much actual sharing going on. Others prefer to call it the on-demand economy, peer-to-peer economy, crowd-based economy, gig economy or collaborative economy.

Uber, Lyft and other e-hailing companies love to say they are "ride-sharing companies," signaling that they are collaborative and not crassly capitalistic. These companies maintain that their drivers share their cars with passengers and use apps to share information about where they are. But many academics and workers in this sector assert that the business model seems less like sharing than like traditional corporate profit-making that happens to use an app.

Rochelle LaPlante, who works for Mechanical Turk, an internet platform for people to post and find piecework jobs, sees public relations spin behind the term "sharing economy." "There's an exchange of money," she said. "It's not really sharing if a person's paying for it."

Her point: If you're living in San Francisco and you want to drive to Palo Alto and take a friend with you (perhaps splitting the cost of gas), that's ride sharing. But if you take an Uber to get to Palo Alto, that seems more like a taxi ride.

Arun Sundararajan, author of the new book "The Sharing Economy: The End of Employment and the Rise of Crowd-Based Capitalism," said he chose that term for his title because so many people use it. Yet Mr. Sundararajan, a professor at New York University's Stern School of Business, actually prefers "crowd-based capitalism," because a crowd of consumers obtains services by connecting, via a platform, with a crowd of suppliers.

MONICA ALMEIDA FOR THE NEW YORK TIMES

Waiting for Uber rides at Los Angeles International Airport. Uber and the like describe themselves as "ride-sharing" companies, but critics call that public relations spin.

In the early 2000s, the sharing economy generally referred to people with underused assets — whether automobiles, homes or vacuum cleaners — who let others "share" them, usually for a fee. Such sharing was viewed not as a business but as a way to promote sustainability.

"The 'sharing economy' phrase has stuck," Professor Sundararajan said, partly because it suggests a personal touch — say, an Airbnb host putting visitors up in a spare bedroom. "There's a connection that people seem to enjoy." (Even though some say that the Airbnb hosts who own a dozen apartments are not really sharing.)

Rachel Botsman, a co-author of "What's Mine Is Yours: The Rise of Collaborative Consumption," says that Uber and the like are not sharing companies. "The Uberfication of everything brings with it confusion about what is true sharing," she wrote on Fast Company's website. To her mind, companies shouldn't be considered part of the sharing economy unless they have a "clear value-driven mission" and their workers are "respected" and "empowered."

Ms. Botsman added that some companies can legitimately be called sharing companies, like Turo (previously called RelayRides), which enables car owners to rent out their unused cars, and BlaBlaCar, which connects riders with car owners planning to drive from one city to another.

With the term "sharing economy" under scrutiny, experts are casting about for substitutes. Miriam A. Cherry, a St. Louis University law professor, recommends the "on-demand economy," but critics say that isn't exact enough, because ordering a pizza by phone can be considered part of an on-demand economy. Others prefer "gig economy," but some assert that phrase isn't suitable for 21st-century app-based companies because gig workers — think jazz musicians — have been around for decades.

Shelby Clark, founder of RelayRides and chief executive of Peers, which advises on-demand companies, prefers "peer-to-peer economy" because individual consumers use a platform to connect with "peer" service providers. But as Professor Sundararajan noted, illegal music and video sharing were once described as peer-to-peer, giving that term a bad connotation.

Some embrace "platform economy," but Geoffrey G. Parker, an engineering professor at Dartmouth and the author of "Platform Revolution," says that name is too broad because it includes giants like Google, Facebook and YouTube. Others like the "app-based on-demand economy" (the Abode economy), the "gig on-demand economy" (the GOD economy) or the "platform on-demand economy" (the POD economy), whose workers could be called pods.

Despite the criticism that "sharing economy" is inaccurate and sounds like corporate spin, Professor Sundararajan says we might be stuck with that description because corporations and the public so often use it. When Silicon Valley and Madison Avenue latch on to a phrase, it's not easy to shake it off.

CHAPTER 2

Transportation

From electric and autonomous cars to space tourism and high-speed commutes, Elon Musk has made a career of disruptive innovation. Creative thinking, a willingness to take risks, and the ability to invest billions of dollars in his own concepts have propelled Musk to the forefront of the race to transform transportation. Whether these innovations will prove profitable remains an open question, but Musk's initiatives have changed the way the public thinks about travel, and forced other companies to follow suit.

When Will Electric Cars Go Mainstream? It May Be Sooner Than You Think

BY BRAD PLUMER | JULY 8, 2017

AS THE WORLD'S automakers place larger bets on electric vehicle technology, many industry analysts are debating a key question: How quickly can plug-in cars become mainstream?

The conventional view holds that electric cars will remain a niche product for many years, plagued by high sticker prices and heavily dependent on government subsidies.

But a growing number of analysts now argue that this pessimism is becoming outdated. A new report from Bloomberg New Energy Finance, a research group, suggests that the price of plug-in cars is falling much faster than expected, spurred by cheaper batteries and aggressive policies promoting zero-emission vehicles in China and Europe.

Between 2025 and 2030, the group predicts, plug-in vehicles will become cost competitive with traditional petroleum-powered cars, even without subsidies and even before taking fuel savings into account. Once that happens, mass adoption should quickly follow.

"Our forecast doesn't hinge on countries adopting stringent new fuel standards or climate policies," said Colin McKerracher, the head of advanced transport analysis at Bloomberg New Energy Finance. "It's an economic analysis, looking at what happens when the upfront cost of electric vehicles reaches parity. That's when the real shift occurs."

If that prediction pans out, it will have enormous consequences for the auto industry, oil markets and the world's efforts to slow global warming.

A BOOST FROM BATTERIES

Last year, plug-in vehicles made up less than 1 percent of new passenger vehicle sales worldwide, held back by high upfront costs. The Chevrolet Bolt, produced by General Motors, sells for about $37,500 before federal tax breaks. With gasoline prices hovering around $2 per gallon, relatively few consumers seem interested.

But there are signs of a shift. Tesla and Volkswagen each have plans to produce more than a million electric vehicles per year by 2025. On Wednesday, Volvo announced that it would phase out the traditional combustion engine and that all of its new models starting in 2019 would be either hybrids or entirely battery-powered.

Skeptics argue that these moves are mostly marginal. Exxon Mobil, which is studying the threat that electric cars could pose to its business model, still expects that plug-in vehicle sales will grow slowly, to just 10 percent of new sales in the United States by 2040, with little impact on global oil use. The federal Energy Information Administration projects a similarly sluggish uptick.

The Bloomberg forecast is far more aggressive, projecting that plug-in hybrids and all-electric vehicles will make up 54 percent of new light-duty sales globally by 2040, outselling their combustion engine counterparts.

The reason? Batteries. Since 2010, the average cost of lithium-ion battery packs has plunged by two-thirds, to around $300 per kilowatt-hour. The Bloomberg report sees that falling to $73 by 2030, without any significant technological breakthroughs, as companies like Tesla increase battery production in massive factories, optimize the design of battery packs and improve chemistries.

For the next decade, the report notes, electric cars will remain reliant on government incentives and sales mandates in places like Europe, China and California. But as automakers introduce a greater variety of models and lower costs, electric cars will reach a point where they can stand on their own.

Still, this outcome is hardly guaranteed. Governments could scale back their incentives before plug-in vehicles become fully competitive — many states are already beginning to tax electric cars. Battery manufacturers could face material shortages or production problems that hinder their ability to slash costs. And an unforeseen technology failure, such as widespread battery fires, could halt progress.

"But we tried to be fairly conservative in our estimate of where battery prices are going," Mr. McKerracher said, "and we don't see barriers to electric vehicles' becoming cost competitive very soon."

Other experts caution that falling battery costs are not the only factor in determining whether electric cars become widespread. Sam Ori, the executive director of the Energy Policy Institute at the University of Chicago, noted, "People don't buy cars based solely on the price tag."

Consumers may remain wary of vehicles with limited range that can take hours to charge. Even though researchers have shown that battery-electric vehicles have sufficient range for many people's daily commuting habits, consumer psychology is still difficult to predict. The report does not, for instance, expect electric vehicles to catch on widely in the pickup-truck market.

Charging infrastructure is another potential barrier. Although cities are starting to build thousands of public charging stations — and

Tesla is working on reducing the time it takes to power a depleted battery — it still takes longer to charge an electric vehicle than it does to refuel a conventional car at the pump.

Many owners charge their cars overnight in their garages, but that is much harder for people living in cities who park their cars on the street.

As a result, the Bloomberg report warns that plug-in vehicles may have a difficult time making inroads in dense urban areas and that infrastructure bottlenecks may slow the growth of electric vehicles after 2040.

Another potential hurdle may be the automakers themselves. While most manufacturers are introducing plug-in models in the United States to comply with stricter fuel-economy standards, they do not always market them aggressively, said Chelsea Sexton, an auto industry consultant who worked on General Motors' electric vehicle program in the 1990s.

Car dealerships also remain reluctant to display and sell electric models, which often require less maintenance and are less profitable for their service departments. Surveys have found that salespeople are often unprepared to pitch the cars.

"We've seen a lot of announcements about electric vehicles, but that doesn't matter much if automakers are just building these cars for compliance and are unenthusiastic about actually marketing them," Ms. Sexton said.

Raw economics may help overcome such barriers, Mr. McKerracher said. He pointed to Norway, where heavy taxes on petroleum-powered vehicles and generous subsidies for electric vehicles have created price parity between the two. As a result, plug-in hybrids and fully electric cars in Norway now make up 37 percent of all new sales, up from 6 percent in 2013.

FIGHTING CLIMATE CHANGE

If Bloomberg's forecast proves correct, it could have sweeping implications for oil markets. The report projects that a sharp rise in electric vehicles would displace eight million barrels of transportation fuel each day. (The world currently consumes around 98 million barrels per day.)

A number of oil companies are now grappling with the prospect of an eventual peak in global demand, with billions of dollars in investments at stake in getting the timing right.

Mass adoption of electric cars could also prove a key strategy in fighting climate change — provided the vehicles are increasingly powered by low-carbon electricity rather than coal. The International Energy Agency has estimated that electric vehicles would have to account for at least 40 percent of passenger vehicle sales by 2040 for the world to have a chance of meeting the climate goals outlined in the Paris agreement, keeping total global warming below 2 degrees Celsius.

Yet the Bloomberg report also shows how much further countries would need to go to cut transportation emissions.

Even with a sharp rise in electric vehicles, the world would still have more traditional petroleum-powered passenger vehicles on the road in 2040 than it does today, and it will take many years to retire existing fleets. And other modes of transportation, like heavy-duty trucking and aviation, will remain stubbornly difficult to electrify without drastic advances in battery technology.

Which means it is still too soon to write an obituary for the internal combustion engine.

Self-Driving Cars Might Need Standards, but Whose?

BY JOHN R. QUAIN | FEB. 23, 2017

THE PC REVOLUTION, the internet boom, the smartphone economy — all were propelled along by a common set of technological standards. So will a standard platform or operating system be necessary to get autonomous cars rolling, too?

"There is certainly no doubt that many carmakers have expressed the idea that a more standardized platform would be attractive," said John Wall, a senior vice president at QNX, which develops software that is used in millions of vehicles today.

Car companies have come to realize that existing in-car systems, with their tangled layers of software and morass of hundreds of embedded processors, are slow and overly complex by today's computing standards. If autonomous cars are ever to become a reality, they will require even more powerful, more fully integrated and upgradable computing platforms, designers say.

"The feedback we hear is that the number of chips, the amount of wire — an Audi has over six miles of wire in it — is excessive," said Danny Shapiro, senior director of automotive at the chip maker Nvidia, which is promoting its own autonomous driving platform.

A more centralized approach could bring huge cost savings by reducing the number of processors used in a car and thus reducing the need for the cabling among those processors. Less wiring would also lower a car's weight to improve fuel economy, Mr. Shapiro said.

Nvidia is currently working with several automakers, including Audi, which plans to have its first self-driving vehicles on the road in 2020.

A common automotive platform could also make it easier to develop new software and safety systems for self-driving cars. "The goal is to reduce the cost of bringing innovation to the mass market," said Eric Montague, a senior director at the speech recognition company Nuance.

Mr. Montague said the challenge today is that every car has a unique constellation of electronic control units, sensors and microphones. The software must be specially tailored to each model.

There is no shortage of companies vying to become the equivalent for self-driving cars of the Windows/Intel standard for PCs. Chip makers like Nvidia — as well as Intel — hope to establish their hardware as the new brains behind autonomous vehicles. Delphi, QNX and Waymo (the former Google self-driving project) are looking to put their software front and center as the operating system of choice. Each wants to sell its own car platform to automakers.

Some auto companies are embracing new partnerships. BMW is working with Intel, Mobileye and Here to bring self-driving cars to the road and plans to start testing such vehicles this year. Ford is working closely with QNX, a BlackBerry subsidiary, on the software needed for the vehicles it is testing. Fiat Chrysler has built a new experimental fleet of minivans for Waymo.

The traditional automotive culture, however, has emphasized independence. And some industry experts point to economic factors that argue against settling on a standard platform. Being dependent on a single vendor can mean higher prices.

"Automakers don't want to rely on Apple or Google," said Glen DeVos, vice president for software and services at Delphi. "But they also don't want to reinvent the wheel all the time."

Emblematic of that carmaker culture is Hyundai, which is mostly going it alone in working on its self-driving entry. The company recently demonstrated how far it has come, ferrying journalists in Las Vegas around in a self-driving version of its Ioniq electric compact car. Hyundai, which likes to emphasize that it even makes its own steel, has developed its own platform, striving for affordability.

"You don't have to use a common system," said Cason Grover, senior group manager for vehicle technology planning innovation at

Hyundai. "And we don't want to go down one path that hinders us in the future from introducing new innovations."

Bosch, which supplies safety and technology systems to automakers, including its own self-parking technology, acknowledges that a single, one-size-fits-all system would be easier to work with. "But it would be a killer for innovation," said Detlef Zerfowski, vice president for automotive system integration at Bosch.

Douglas L. Davis of Intel, recently charged with spearheading that company's new self-driving car platform, Go, said, "Given the amount of computing power necessary for autonomous driving, we think it can benefit from greater commonality and predictable interfaces."

"Mobileye already has the computer vision, for example," he said. "So if the technology is good, why re-engineer it and take two to three years to get it into a product?"

Which design philosophy one chooses can have significant repercussions when it comes to the security of robotic cars, evoking visions of hackers causing mayhem by crashing cars and trucks into each other at highway speeds. It's a problem engineers are keenly aware of.

"Having a common platform could have a downside," Mr. Wall at QNX acknowledged. "If there's a vulnerability in one car, it could mean there's a vulnerability in every car."

Conversely, Mr. Wall pointed out that de facto software standards mean that more programmers are focused on making those systems as secure as possible, versus having only a few coders working on a single, narrowly used program.

But by developing as much of the technology as possible themselves, some automakers believe they can solve problems more quickly.

"A side benefit of controlling the entire thing," said Mr. Grover at Hyundai, "is that we know everything that's going on."

A lack of standards and a diversity of self-driving systems does present one other obvious challenge: Variety is not a virtue when cars must interact predictably with human drivers — and other robotic vehicles — to guarantee safety.

Riding in Hyundai's self-driving Ioniq, for example, is like taking a Sunday drive with your grandmother. The car is extremely adept at staying squarely in its lane without ping-ponging back and forth, but it is also cautious in the extreme, stopping nine feet short of crosswalks and stubbornly refusing to go forward if a pedestrian looks poised to step off the sidewalk. It is behavior that can ignite road rage in nearby human drivers.

By comparison, Delphi's test car, which uses an Intel computing platform installed in an Audi Q5, is more aggressive. It can easily merge into highway traffic and negotiate complex intersections. However, it treats pedestrians with less deference, taking right-hand corners more quickly — even though pedestrians may be contemplating entering the crosswalk.

"There's a big difference in the algorithms and even sensor choices being used," Mr. Grover said, which can affect how collision-prevention and lane-keeping systems work. When autonomous cars do hit the road, he said, you could have a fair amount of variation in how they behave.

"There are quite a few different approaches to creating autonomous systems," said Ralf Herrtwich of Here, which is making high-resolution maps for the next generation of vehicles. Mr. Herrtwich said the necessary standards might come not from the car platform itself, though, but from the communications side.

In order to avoid accidents down the road and conditions like black ice that a car's sensors cannot detect, self-driving vehicles will have to share information with each other, through so-called V2V or vehicle-to-vehicle communication. The National Highway Traffic Safety Administration has proposed that V2V equipment be installed in all cars in the future.

Indeed, there are already cars like the 2017 BMW 5 Series that can broadcast information about road hazards over a cellular connection, but only other BMWs can make use of the warnings.

Technology suppliers, platform vendors and automakers acknowledge that self-driving cars are still in their infancy and that as the vehicles mature, standards will be forthcoming.

Most car manufacturers are still struggling just to establish standards across their own models and brands, Mr. DeVos of Delphi said.

"Once that happens," he said, "then we can talk about how to work across different companies."

Uber Strikes Deal With Volvo to Bring Self-Driving Cars to Its Network

BY MIKE ISAAC | NOV. 20, 2017

SAN FRANCISCO — No one knows what the future of self-driving cars will look like, or how long it will take to get there. But every major player in the field is striking partnerships to be ready for the day when autonomous vehicles finally become mainstream.

That includes Uber, which on Monday announced a new deal with Volvo. Under the agreement, Uber plans to purchase as many as 24,000 self-driving Volvos once the technology is production-ready, putting the vehicles into its extensive ride-hailing network.

"Everything we're doing right now is about building autonomous vehicles at scale," Jeff Miller, Uber's head of automotive alliances, said in an interview. "We don't know exactly how an autonomous world will look. But we know that we want to be the platform that's at the center of it, from a ride-sharing standpoint."

The deal is an extension of an agreement Uber made with Volvo nearly two years ago, when the ride-hailing company started its research and development efforts in autonomous vehicles in earnest. Uber has worked with third-party component manufacturers to build software and hardware for driverless cars, then worked closely with Volvo to outfit the automaker's XC90 vehicles with the technology.

But the new deal vastly increases the number of Volvo driverless cars that Uber can work with, showing the scope of its ambitions.

Volvo, which is based in Sweden and owned by Geely Automobile Holdings of China, said in a statement that Volvo and Uber were contributing $300 million to the project.

From automakers like Ford, Tesla and General Motors to technology companies like Google, Uber and Lyft, titans of the transportation industry are racing to gain an edge in a future of autonomous vehicles. Each of the players has approached the issue differently. Automakers like G.M. and Ford have spent billions buying software-based start-ups to work on integrating driverless technology into their vehicles. Tesla has long offered a hybrid version of self-driving software in its vehicles, and recently debuted an electric, nearly autonomous semi truck that it expects to hit the road in the next few years.

Uber has done most of its work in research and development in-house instead of teaming up with multiple manufacturers, as has been the case with Lyft, Uber's largest rival in the United States. In particular, Uber has invested in its Advanced Technologies Group, home to hundreds of engineers in Pittsburgh, where it is doing much of its autonomous vehicle research.

"The only way we could control our own destiny was to work with this technology that had the potential to disrupt our business, and have direct involvement in the creation of it," Mr. Miller said. "We couldn't afford to be on the outside looking in. We have to be in the game."

Some of Uber's work in self-driving cars has run into hurdles. The company has been fighting a lawsuit from Waymo, Google's onetime autonomous car business, over stolen trade secrets.

Uber has expanded its partnerships over the past year, striking deals with automakers like Daimler to bring autonomous cars onto the ride-hailing company's network.

Mr. Miller said that Uber would own and operate fleets of its own vehicles purchased from partners like Volvo, but that there was no one-size-fits-all approach, so it would also allow other self-driving vehicles on its network.

Self-Driving Uber Car Kills Pedestrian in Arizona, Where Robots Roam

BY DAISUKE WAKABAYASHI | MARCH 19, 2018

SAN FRANCISCO — Arizona officials saw opportunity when Uber and other companies began testing driverless cars a few years ago. Promising to keep oversight light, they invited the companies to test their robotic vehicles on the state's roads.

Then on Sunday night, an autonomous car operated by Uber — and with an emergency backup driver behind the wheel — struck and killed a woman on a street in Tempe, Ariz. It was believed to be the first pedestrian death associated with self-driving technology. The company quickly suspended testing in Tempe as well as in Pittsburgh, San Francisco and Toronto.

The accident was a reminder that self-driving technology is still in the experimental stage, and governments are still trying to figure out how to regulate it.

Uber, Waymo and a long list of tech companies and automakers have begun to expand testing of their self-driving vehicles in cities around the country. The companies say the cars will be safer than regular cars simply because they take easily distracted humans out of the driving equation. But the technology is still only about a decade old, and just now starting to experience the unpredictable situations that drivers can face.

It was not yet clear if the crash in Arizona will lead other companies or state regulators to slow the rollout of self-driving vehicles on public roads.

Much of the testing of autonomous cars has taken place in a piecemeal regulatory environment. Some states, like Arizona, have taken a lenient approach to regulation. Arizona officials wanted to lure companies working on self-driving technology out of neighboring California,

CAITLIN O'HARA FOR THE NEW YORK TIMES

A woman crossing Mill Avenue at its intersection with Curry Road in Tempe, Ariz. A pedestrian was struck and killed by a self-driving Uber vehicle at the intersection the night before.

where regulators had been less receptive.

But regulators in California and elsewhere have become more accommodating lately. In April, California is expected to follow Arizona's lead and allow companies to test cars without a person in the driver's seat.

Federal policymakers have also considered a lighter touch. A Senate bill, if passed, would free autonomous-car makers from some existing safety standards and pre-empt states from creating their own vehicle safety laws. Similar legislation has been passed in the House. The Senate version has passed a committee vote but hasn't reached a full floor vote.

"This tragic incident makes clear that autonomous vehicle technology has a long way to go before it is truly safe for the passengers, pedestrians, and drivers who share America's roads," said Senator Richard Blumenthal, Democrat of Connecticut.

The Uber car, a Volvo XC90 sport utility vehicle outfitted with the company's sensing system, was in autonomous mode with a human safety driver at the wheel but carrying no passengers when it struck Elaine Herzberg, a 49-year-old woman, on Sunday around 10 p.m.

Sgt. Ronald Elcock, a Tempe police spokesman, said during a news conference that a preliminary investigation showed that the vehicle was moving around 40 miles per hour when it struck Ms. Herzberg, who was walking with her bicycle on the street. He said it did not appear as though the car had slowed down before impact and that the Uber safety driver had shown no signs of impairment. The weather was clear and dry.

Uber said it would work with the police.

"Our hearts go out to the victim's family," an Uber spokeswoman, Sarah Abboud, said in a statement. "We are fully cooperating with local authorities in their investigation of this incident."

Tempe, with its dry weather and wide roads, was considered an ideal place to test autonomous vehicles. In 2015, Arizona officials declared the state a regulation-free zone in order to attract testing operations from companies like Uber, Waymo and Lyft.

"We needed our message to Uber, Lyft and other entrepreneurs in Silicon Valley to be that Arizona was open to new ideas," Doug Ducey, Arizona's governor, said in an interview in June 2017.

Using an executive order, Mr. Ducey opened the state to testing of autonomous vehicles that had safety drivers at the wheel, ready to take over in an emergency. He updated that mandate earlier this month to allow testing of unmanned self-driving cars, noting that a "business-friendly and low regulatory environment" had helped the state's economy.

Even when an Uber self-driving car and another vehicle collided in Tempe in March 2017, city police and Mr. Ducey said that extra safety regulations weren't necessary; the other driver was at fault, not the self-driving vehicle.

But on Monday, Mark Mitchell, Tempe's mayor, called Uber's decision to suspend autonomous vehicle testing a "responsible step" and cautioned people from drawing conclusions prematurely. Daniel

Scarpinato, a spokesman for Mr. Ducey, said the updated order from the governor "provides enhanced enforcement measures and clarity on responsibility in these accidents."

In California, where testing without a backup driver was just weeks away from being permitted, Jessica Gonzalez, a spokeswoman for the state Department of Motor Vehicles, said officials were in the process of gathering more information about the Tempe crash. Waymo, Lyft and Cruise, an autonomous vehicle company owned by General Motors, did not respond to requests for comment.

In a news release, the National Transportation Safety Board said it was sending a team of four investigators to examine "the vehicle's interaction with the environment, other vehicles and vulnerable road users such as pedestrians and bicyclists."

Most testing of driverless cars occurs with a safety driver in the front seat who is available to take over if something goes wrong. It can be challenging, however, to take control of a fast-moving vehicle.

California requires companies to report the number of instances when human drivers are forced to take over for the autonomous vehicle, called "disengagements."

Between December 2016 and November 2017, Waymo's self-driving cars drove about 350,000 miles and human drivers retook the wheel 63 times — an average of about 5,600 miles between every disengagement. Uber has not been testing its self-driving cars long enough in California to be required to release its disengagement numbers.

Researchers working on autonomous technology have struggled with how to teach the systems to adjust for unpredictable human driving or behavior. Still, most researchers believe self-driving cars will ultimately be more safe than their human counterparts.

In 2016, 37,461 people died in traffic-related accidents in the United States, according to the National Highway Traffic Safety Administration. That amounts to 1.18 fatalities per 100 million vehicle miles traveled in 2016.

Waymo, which has been testing autonomous vehicles on public roads since 2009 when it was Google's self-driving car project, has said its cars have driven more than 5 million miles while Uber's cars have covered 3 million miles.

In 2016, a man driving his Tesla using Autopilot, the car company's self-driving feature, died on a state highway in Florida when his car crashed into a tractor-trailer that was crossing the road. Federal regulators later ruled there were no defects in the system to cause the accident.

But the crash in Tempe will draw attention among the general public to self-driving cars, said Michael Bennett, an associate research professor at Arizona State University who has been looking into how people respond to driverless cars and artificial intelligence.

"We've imagined an event like this as a huge inflection point for the technology and the companies advocating for it," he said. "They're going to have to do a lot to prove that the technology is safe."

REBEKAH ZEMANSKY CONTRIBUTED REPORTING IN TEMPE, ARIZ. CECILIA KANG CONTRIBUTED REPORTING IN WASHINGTON D.C. AND CADE METZ CONTRIBUTED IN SAN FRANCISCO.

Uber's Self-Driving Trucks Hit the Highway, but Not Local Roads

BY DAISUKE WAKABAYASHI | MARCH 6, 2018

SAN FRANCISCO — More than a year after Uber's self-driving trucks made their first commercial delivery — 2,000 cases of Budweiser beer on a 120-mile hop in Colorado — the company says it has taken its robot big rigs to the highways of Arizona.

Uber said on Tuesday that its self-driving trucks had been carrying cargo on highways in Arizona for commercial freight customers over the past few months. The trucks operate with a licensed truck driver at the wheel, ready to take over in the case of an emergency. But Uber said the eventual goal was to eliminate human drivers inside the cab.

In a video, Uber laid out its vision for the future of trucking — tapping autonomous systems to navigate long highway hauls and relying on human drivers to handle shorter drives, like the final few miles to a customer's loading dock.

The ride-hailing service is one of the first companies to begin commercializing self-driving trucks, integrating — albeit slowly — the technology into its shipment-booking service, Uber Freight.

At the heart of Uber's vision are transfer hubs where trucks can pick up and drop off trailers. At those locations, autonomous trucks would grab trailers for long-haul drives, while human drivers would grab ones earmarked for closer delivery — with Uber's network meshing the supply and demand of both behind the scenes.

Uber's self-driving truck emerged from its 2016 acquisition of Otto, an autonomous trucking start-up founded by a former Google engineer. The acquisition was at the heart of an intellectual property lawsuit against Uber that was brought by Waymo, the self-driving car unit from Google's parent company, Alphabet. The two sides settled the case last month.

While that legal case dragged out, the company continued to refine its driverless truck technology to find its place in an increasingly crowded field. Waymo has also said it is considering using its driverless car technology for trucks, while Tesla said it plans to introduce an electric truck with a self-driving mode built in.

Trucking is a natural target for automation. In theory, automated trucks can stay on the road longer than those with human drivers and, over time, are expected to be less prone to accidents because they don't get sleepy or distracted. Eventually, these factors are expected to make self-driving trucks a cheaper alternative.

"We think self-driving technology has tremendous potential to solve some of the big problems that the trucking industry has today," said Alden Woodrow, the product manager for Uber's self-driving truck unit.

Uber launched Uber Freight, an app that matches truckers and trucking companies with loads to haul, in May 2017. In a business model that is similar to its ride-hailing service, Uber doesn't actually handle the deliveries but works behind the scenes to create a marketplace for truckers and shippers.

The company said it was working out of two primary transfer hubs in Arizona — one in Sanders near the border with New Mexico and another in Topock near the California border.

Uber isn't saying much about its self-driving trucks. It won't disclose how many trucks it is using, how many miles they've driven or how often the human safety drivers had to intervene and assist the autonomous system. It is also not revealing many details about how the transfer hubs would work — including what they would look like, where they would be located and how the company planned to roll them out.

When it comes to the politically sensitive question of whether Uber's technology will eventually eliminate trucking jobs, the company walks a fine line. For now, Uber said it believed the introduction of self-driving trucks would bring about more driving jobs, not fewer, in part because of greater demand as delivery costs fall. However, the nature of a trucker's job may change — becoming something akin to a parcel delivery driver, shuttling trailers between the hub and local destinations.

While autonomous systems may one day be able to do everything a human truck driver does, Uber said it was not training its trucks to do it all, like back up to a loading dock or navigate around a busy industrial area.

“That is beyond the window of what we’re looking at,” Mr. Woodrow said. Uber is choosing to “focus the development of our technology on the highway only.”

Full Tilt: When 100% of Cars Are Autonomous

BY THE NEW YORK TIMES | NOV. 8, 2017

So, wow, imagine we get there: total autonomy. Manual driving is outlawed. Our cars are better drivers than we ever were. And not only that, they coordinate with one another in an elegant choreography, threading through traffic with inches to spare. Parking becomes parkland, because no cars ever stay still for long; they stop only to recharge themselves as needed. If you choose, you can just hang out at home and let the robocars bring you everything you need. But even if that future does arrive, it would come with a trunkful of nagging questions. What does it feel like to live in that world? And how does 21st-century society — which has been built, in ways large and small, around human drivers — change and reconfigure when they all become mere riders? In the pages that follow, we begin to wonder at some answers.

CITIES WITHOUT SIGNS

BY CLIVE THOMPSON

STREET SIGNAGE IS the iconography of the automobile age. It's like highly functional pop art: silhouettes of schoolchildren, white arrows, rectangular cries of WRONG WAY and, most central of all, the ubiquitous stoplight. The traffic light might be the first part of that iconographic world to be transformed, or vanish altogether, once we are fully in the age of autonomous cars. Robots, after all, won't need signs to optimize the way they move through urban landscapes.

Urban-transportation experts have been busily creating computer simulations to show how this might work. In one model, each crossroads would have an "intersection manager," a computer that senses the approaching traffic and uses wireless communication to talk to the oncoming cars. When each self-driving car is perhaps 300 yards away, it sends a request to the intersection manager — to turn right, say, or to move on through. The intersection manager then does an on-the-fly calculation to route that vehicle most efficiently, like an omnipotent and tireless traffic cop.

The result? A ballet of cars whizzing and weaving past one another in the intersection. Some slow down as they approach; others pass straight through. But crucially, compared with today's intersections, many fewer cars come to a complete halt.

This could significantly speed up traffic throughout an entire city. Peter Stone, a computer scientist at the University of Texas at Austin who works with one model, has found that the "delay" time at intersections shrinks remarkably. "Right now, it takes me an average of 20 minutes to get to work, but with autonomous-car intersections, it might be half that time," he says. Safety would be enhanced, too: Forty-three percent of car crashes in the United States occur at intersections, and Stone predicts that robot vehicles would crash only if there was a mechanical error. Better yet, autonomous intersections could produce an estimated 20 to 50 percent less carbon dioxide, because there would be fewer idling cars and jack-rabbit starts. "That's the most expensive and most polluting part of driving," says Remi Tachet des Combes, a mathematician who created robot-intersection models while at the Massachusetts Institute of Technology.

For the human passenger, though, a robotized intersection could be mildly terrifying — like flying through a crowded asteroid belt, trusting the A.I. to find the right path. "At first I think it will be freaky," Stone admits. "Some people will need the window darkened so they don't freak out." But in the long run, we'll probably shrug, get used to it and barely look up from our games of Candy Crush as we zip through. And pedestrians? They would probably push a button at the intersection to request their turn — or even use a smartphone app.

More subtly unsettling, however, might be the spectacle of a city devoid of stoplights. Indeed, devoid of all major street signs: no huge billboards across highways naming the exits, no complex merge instructions. Those signs are expensive to build and maintain. They're designed for humans, and GPS-brained robots don't need them to know where they're going. Certainly, human pedestrians and cyclists will still need guideposts, but as Stone suspects, far fewer, and smaller, ones.

A world with almost no street signs would feel strange. It could make a city less cluttered and more attractive. But it might also leave us feeling unmoored. Social critics worry that GPS has already eroded our knowledge of the city; some studies have found that the more we rely on devices, the less we deeply intuit where we are and how to navigate on our own. "We become more helpless," as Greg Milner, the author of "Pinpoint," a history of GPS, told me. If robots rule the roads, we might get where we're going a lot more quickly — but end up not knowing precisely where we are.

CLIVE THOMPSON IS THE AUTHOR OF "SMARTER THAN YOU THINK: HOW TECHNOLOGY IS CHANGING OUR MINDS FOR THE BETTER."

PICTURING THE SELF-DRIVING CITY

BY ANNA WIENER

MARSHALL BROWN, an associate professor of architecture at the Illinois Institute of Technology, recently traveled to Ann Arbor, Mich., to visit the Mcity Test Facility, the University of Michigan's 32-acre testing ground for automated vehicles. Mcity, which looks like a soundstage of a midcentury suburb, is a simulator: It has no actual residents. Still, Brown found it "bizarre and frankly frightening" that it looked as though the track had been designed almost entirely by transportation experts, not urban planners or architects. He identified it as part of a larger problem: As technologists imagine the driverless world, they seem to be doing so with a distinct lack of imagination.

Brown is a creator of the Driverless City Project, an interdisciplinary research initiative at I.I.T. that takes a playful, rigorous approach to envisioning the fully autonomous future. The project helps participants generate various situations for a city in order to determine how autonomous cars will fit into the picture. Central to the project is a "mind map" representing the group's research, organized into four areas of impact: street space, parking space, commuter space and delivery space. The map, as well as other tools — including a set of large tokens for scenario building, like a tarot deck for urbanists — is meant to encourage others to be ambitious and creative about the world in which they want to live. "We should write the future," Brown says, "rather than trying to predict it."

Brown has found two prevalent attitudes when it comes to self-driving vehicles: either an active but unimaginative approach, rushing to build robots to accommodate the world as it is now, or a totally passive approach, a sort of "wait and see." The first, he says, is characteristic of the tech industry; the second, of the public sector. "I hear too much surrendering in the question about our future right now," he adds. "Just surrendering to Google or Amazon, or surrendering to your phone, or surrendering to a driverless car. We should not surrender."

One way to stave off surrender, Brown believes, is to invite more diverse thinkers, like architects and urban planners, into the process of imagining and designing the autonomous future. (He also listed sociologists, fiction writers, Buddhist monks, poets and rabbis as useful stakeholders.) The current discourse around the future of autonomous vehicles is centered on "technologically deterministic fantasies," Brown says. He's concerned that technological values — like logic, predictability and efficiency — will be erroneously imposed upon the built environment, leading to urban spaces that fail to take into account delight, pleasure or human connection. "A society is cultural, and political, and aesthetic, and about desires — it's not just how you solve problems," he says. "They're going to need more than just software engineers working on it."

As an architect, Brown is especially attuned to the unlocked aesthetic potential of urban environments. Today's visual clutter, necessary for keeping human-driven cars as nonlethal as possible, could be eradicated. It is critical, in his view, to consider the beauty and quality of the world that self-driving cars could bring.

It's worth considering, then, where cars will go when people don't need them. "What happens when a car can park itself anywhere?" Brown asks. He hypothesizes that parking, if performed robotically, could become “a negative externality, not unlike that of a trash dump,” should developers repurpose garages and parking lots for more lucrative uses. (Why look for parking in Greenwich Village if the car can park itself on the edge of New Jersey?) In the Midwest, he speculates, deindustrialized cities with waning property values could even be bought wholesale and transformed into vast, flat parking lots — a future that he deemed plausible, if “too dystopian,” in no small part because of the likelihood that it would be pushed upon lower-income communities. On the other hand, those same communities could benefit from increased mobility and access to employment.

Brown is also considering the changes to storage: If robotic trucks constantly roam our landscape, will warehouses be abandoned? He’s focused on the changing needs and desires of a human driver. To accommodate an autonomous, cross-country route, truck cabs, he speculates, may need to expand according to a driver’s needs, perhaps going so far as to resemble a microapartment.

An emphasis (or lack thereof) on efficiency also addresses the temporal dimension of cities: It favors — or facilitates — a working lifestyle in which there is never enough time. In a future of increased automation and accessibility, work culture may begin to shift; labor, and its attendant time constraints, may no longer be central to the urban experience. Brown envisions the possibility of a hands-free commute that opens up space for socializing — “an interior social world.” Riders could chat with people in adjacent cars or simply take the opportunity to watch the world go by. (A more cynical take on this, he says, is that the hands-free commute will simply increase the demands on workers, as the car becomes an extension of the home office — a WeWork on wheels.)

Second-order effects of autonomous vehicles tend to get lost in the techno-utopian chatter, but there seems to be an increasing awareness that self-driving cars won’t just arrive in cities; they’ll change them too. Some tech companies are beginning to get into data-driven city-building, a movement largely galvanized by the seeming inevitability of autonomous vehicles. Last year, Y Combinator announced a research initiative, New Cities, that aimed to study how to build a metropolis entirely from scratch. In mid-October, Sidewalk Labs, an Alphabet subsidiary, announced that it will redevelop a 12-acre strip along Toronto's waterfront, called Quayside, which will integrate technology across the human experience. The vehicles it is planning to accommodate will be shared, electric and self-driving.

Power and control over autonomous-vehicle technology is already concentrated in the hands of a small few: If a company like Uber or Alphabet controls the dominant transportation infrastructure, you need not live in an intentional community like Quayside to feel as though your city is becoming a company town. Brown is wary of the smart-cities initiative, and he resents the efforts of technology companies to fully saturate the human — and urban — experience. "A city is not a problem to be solved," he says. "A city is a cultural construct, even though it involves the deployment of technologies. A city is not science alone."

ANNA WIENER IS A WRITER BASED IN SAN FRANCISCO.

THE AUGMENTED-REALITY WINDSHIELD

BY FERRIS JABR

FOR OBVIOUS REASONS, our present-day cars are designed for keen observation of the outside world, offering a nearly panoramic view of the road and landscape through panels of glass. The parade of images flitting past a car's windows can be exhilarating or can induce a kind of pleasurable trance. By virtue of being transparent and inert, however, windows are inherently limited. Although we have begun to augment the car's field of vision with new layers of information — phones suction-cupped to the windshield, or GPS built into the dashboard — there is still so much useful knowledge just out of reach. Today's windows allow you to scope out a parking spot or search for that tiny cafe with the faded sign, but they can't help you find them. Nor can they show you exactly where that highway exit will lead or identify the odd building you just passed.

Tomorrow's could. Unlike Google Glass — which awkwardly placed screens where they didn't need to be — a car already requires a membrane between passengers and their environment. Why not turn that typically passive barrier into a dynamic canvas? Ordinary windows could be replaced with holographic glass or an advanced semitranslucent liquid-crystal display. They could anticipate our needs and instantaneously display weather forecasts, reviews of nearby restaurants and hotels, details about popular tourist attractions — and warnings about miserable tourist traps.

As the technology improves and people become more comfortable obscuring their surroundings, your windows could begin to overlay a vast digital diorama onto passing scenery. Passengers would no longer have to wonder about the identity of a landmark and scramble to look it up on their phones. Instead, the car itself, wired with artificial intelligence, plugged into sophisticated mapping technology and equipped with magic eyes, would instantaneously recognize, annotate and augment its surroundings. A mountain, desert or coastline could become an interactive infographic, peeling away the physical surface of the earth to reveal hidden layers of geology. A self-directed double-decker bus ambling through London could rearrange the city like a Lego set, refashioning streets and buildings to illuminate the capital's rich history. Early television sets made the distant accessible; the self-driving car could reveal the invisible in the immediate.

As exciting as such possibilities are, recent history suggests plenty of reasons to temper our optimism. When windows double as screens, we will have the opportunity to gaze at the world anew through richly animated portals. Alternatively — and perhaps more realistically — we could end up staring into larger versions of our phones, distracting ourselves with email, mindless games and the infinite bazaar of the internet. The potential of the autonomous vehicle is to help us interact with our environment in ways never before possible. The temptation is to turn ever more inward, exchanging the physical world for yet another simulation.

Either way, self-driving cars with ubiquitous screens will inevitably bring all the familiar drawbacks of digital media onto the open road. Taxi TV in New York City is just a preview of the potential nightmare. What if the price for enchanted windows of the future is a nauseating kaleidoscope of advertisements, vapid movie reviews and contextless late-night jokes? Rather than learning about the hidden history of your surroundings, you may very well learn only about two-for-one cricket tacos in the food truck a lane over, homeowner's insurance for the Anthropocene or the sale on microdrones at a nearby mall. Don't want ads? No problem. You can upgrade to a premium account.

FERRIS JABR IS A WRITER BASED IN PORTLAND, ORE.

THE SEIZURE OF COMMUTING TIME

BY RAHAWA HAILE

ONE BIG QUESTION about the driverless car will be who gets to own our new wealth of free time. Will it remain with commuters — or will corporations expect them to tap into the office as their vehicles ferry them there? While the potential for hours of unplugged leisure exists, the way we currently fill our downtime leads me to believe that some form of digital immersion will take precedence, as bosses expect employees to work on their way to and from work. It wouldn't be surprising to see the remaining minimum-wage positions in the rapidly automating food industry go to those who have access to driverless cars; use their cars for deliveries while they work, and you get two employees for the price of one.

It's tricky. On their surface, driverless cars will take some of the mess out of living, but they can also take the living where they don't want to go, both psychologically and physically. Some car interiors might more closely resemble cubicles. Or cells. Will private employers surveil workers in order to control off-duty behavior? It's also easy to conceive of a future where newly created infrastructure, explicitly dedicated to automated vehicles, will enable people with the means to own the cars to avoid the people without.

We should be wary of any technology that allows those with power to distance themselves even further from society.

RAHAWA HAILE IS AN ERITREAN-AMERICAN WRITER OF SHORT STORIES AND ESSAYS.

NONSTOP TEENAGE PARTY

BY GEOFF MANAUGH

IN A SHORT ESSAY published in 1970, the British architect David Greene suggested that his colleagues pay more attention to cars. "A traffic jam is a collection of rooms," he explained, and "so is a car park — they are really instantly formed and constantly changing communities." It was a memorable observation that nonetheless would surprise few teenagers, who long ago embraced the transformative notion that cars are not just rooms, but rooms they can control.

Autonomous cars will once again transform teenage life. Anab Jain, a founder of the design studio Superflux, says the ritual requirements of teenage socializing will inspire "a new range of acts and services that help you obfuscate your car's identity or your own data." Instead of trying to roll back the odometer on the family car à la Ferris Bueller, teenagers hoping to roam the city, free from parental view, might trick it into recording destinations they didn't really visit. "The whole notion of freedom will change," Jain says, even as some of the destinations remain familiar. Dark streets or quiet state parks where GPS doesn't reach would be the coolest sites of all.

The question of when, exactly, the party has started will also become an intriguing one: After all, each car is a room unto itself. The Situationist International, a loose group of artists, political agitators and heavy drinkers who roamed the streets of Paris and other cities in the 1960s, treating them as arenas for detours and debauchery, offers some clues about how such rooms could be transformed. "I only ever hear self-driving cars talked about as a functional solution to the problem of getting from A to B," says McKenzie Wark, the author of a history of the Situationists called "The Beach Beneath the Street."

(The title is a reference to the sand that was revealed when protesters picked up cobblestones from the Paris streets to throw at the police.) Wark imagines these machines rolling out of the factory with more radical settings hard-wired into their operating systems. "A hybrid of the self-driving car and, say, Grindr could bring a whole new meaning to the concept of cruising," Wark suggests. "There should be a 'scenic route' setting, a 'random' setting, a 'surprise me' setting. Or maybe 'mystery destination,' which whisks you — and algorithmically chosen others — to an undisclosed location. Algorithmic chicken for teenage drivers, where you drive head-on toward another car — then magically swerve off at the last minute."

Unlike today's cars, autonomous cars can also be made to swarm together, creating somewhat of a paradox: a moving traffic jam. Once the swarm is formed, proximity algorithms could mine social-media profiles to arrange like-minded clusters, while enabling "shuffle mode" might one day be the equivalent of texting a friend to rescue you from the boring guy in the corner. Aspiring D.J.s will rely on software to assemble self-driving cars into the ideal configuration for louder bass. Couples armed with GPS jammers — the future's perfect Valentine's Day gift — will quietly steer strangers away, creating a halo of romantic privacy around their makeout sessions. If all else fails, hit "skip" to be transported to an entirely new party.

Hidden beneath the hormone haze of future block parties, new opportunities for cultural pranks and political protest will emerge. Rather than throw cobblestones, protesters could quickly jam the streets to show political solidarity or organize a strike. With the right programming skills, they might be able to shut down a whole city just by blocking a few crucial nodes. They could even open the streets back up to foot traffic, remaking them as a space for celebration. Then, of course, when it's time to go home, all those dull factory presets, optimized for safety and efficiency, will finally come into their own — no designated driver necessary.

GEOFF MANAUGH IS THE AUTHOR OF "A BURGLAR'S GUIDE TO THE CITY."

YOUR AUTONOMOUS DEALER

BY JAMIE LAUREN KEILES

DRUG DEALERS TEND to choose cars at the extremes — on the one hand a cocaine-white G-Wagen, on the other a '98 Toyota Tercel. Each suggests a kind of shady guarantee that the self-driving car isn't likely to sustain. Like most new stuff from Silicon Valley, the autonomous car is bound to be cute — a gumdrop whip fit for a Pixar protagonist. Hardly what you dream of when you're trying to score. If drugs are still cool, they'll have stayed that way in part because of their illicitness and the mild supply-line chaos that brute fact engenders: the inconsistent product, unreliable hookups and hours spent waiting for the dealer to arrive. Self-driving cars will succeed only by reducing and avoiding such chaos as much as possible. If these two industries are ever to play nice, then the success of one will come at the cost of the cool-guy reputation of the other.

In the self-driving future, a weed transaction will begin the same as always — by texting your dealer in search of "tree," or by casually asking if he wants to "hang out." En route to another customer's house, he will text back immediately, freed from the imposition of two hands on the wheel. Memories of waiting impatiently on a flaky dealer will recede as his car appears on your app, predicting arrival time down to the minute. Watch as his vehicle weaves around school zones, or is maybe flagged and pulled over by the police. The new possibilities for surveillance are endless.

In any case, if he makes it to your house, it is likely that he will emerge from his self-driving pod in a sweatshirt for a company with a name like TōkTaxi or Gangl.ly or Lyft'd. As weed begins to trend toward legality, we've already seen such standing-desk branding start to creep into the stoner vernacular. A scan down PC Magazine's "15 Blazing Hot Weed Tech Companies to Watch" reveals Tokken (a blockchain system for dealers), MassRoots (a stoner social network) and Eaze (the obligatory "Uber for weed"). In this new age of cannabis, the only thing that moves faster than the tech is the rate at which smoking itself becomes corny.

But cringe-worthy orthography is not the only thing that this self-driven industry will inherit from Silicon Valley. In the age of semi-autonomous cars, dealers will be forced to file 1099s, sharing their profits as lowly subcontractors. As in the time when dealers drove themselves, this fleet of buddies-for-hire will offer five to 10 minutes of humanity-affirming chitchat. Unlike preautonomous dealers, they will plead that you tweet their referral codes in order to receive a complimentary edible.

This, of course, is one good reason to strive for fully autonomous drugmobiles. The driverless vehicle eliminates small talk, supplying your fix directly from the glove box with a personalized passcode, à la Amazon Locker. With no human body attached to the cargo, suppliers will seek to move harder drugs, in bigger quantities, potentially unleashing a new set of problems. The narc, a liability throughout all of human history, isn't likely to go anywhere soon. Self-driving cars will scan for hazards in the street but will also pick up telltale signs of an informant: nervous twitches, too-enthusiastic slang. A customer might even be asked to answer a question like, "Are you a cop?" (Because, as all drug dealers know, a real cop has to say yes, even to an A.I.) It is likely that a database of narcs will be compiled, and inevitably, this database of narcs will be hacked. Millions of Americans will be exposed as poseurs — a social problem tragically immune to disruption.

JAMIE LAUREN KEILES IS A WRITER IN NEW YORK.

POLICING WITH NO TICKETS

BY GARETH COOK

THE TEMPTATION IS the greatest on nights when the evening rush seems to congeal around the car, and she just wants to be home. She waits until she has left downtown (too many traffic towers), and then, with a few taps to a screen, she goes for it. Chinese software hacks come well recommended, and it's soon clear why: The car picks up speed and begins to weave through the slower traffic — pleasingly aggressive but more sure in its lines, with less lurching, than the typical Russian black-market goods. She returns to her movie, but before long she hears a chime and a grating alert: "Traffic ticket assessed." She spots a police car speeding past, a quad drone fixed to the roof, as her own vehicle reverts to its factory settings and rejoins the docile march of the lemmings.

In the coming world of ubiquitous self-driving, it will just be you, the open road and the vast apparatus of the nanny state. Cars won't readily violate traffic laws and may well be legally required to report on their owners. Ignore that burned-out headlight for too long, and the overnight software update may include a virtual boot.

Traffic tickets bring in billions of dollars annually, so all those well-behaved cars will have an economic impact. Governments that have historically viewed traffic citations as an extractive industry (Ferguson, Mo., say, or the State of California) will have no choice but to find alternatives. Far more consequential, for both the police and their communities, will be the death of the routine traffic stop. The Supreme Court has ruled that law enforcement may stop any car, whatever its true motive, as long as an infraction is observed. Human drivers can't get far without breaking the letter of the traffic law, so the pretexts come easy. If officers then spot a dozen laptops stacked on the back seat, they can ask questions. Yet this broad, virtually unchecked power to stop has led to charges of racial profiling. (A recent linguistic analysis of bodycam footage from Oakland, Calif., for example, concluded that officers spoke "with consistently less respect toward black versus white community members.") With pretexts largely automated away, these kinds of interactions will be rare. "The self-driving car," says Elizabeth Joh, a professor at the U.C. Davis School of Law, "will come to be seen as a civil rights issue."

The police will have lost an important investigative tool, but the government will have gained new surveillance possibilities. Cars will sweep up vast amounts of data about their surroundings and their occupants, including 24/7 GPS trails. (An important Fourth Amendment case being heard this fall, Carpenter v. United States, will decide whether the government needs a warrant to gain access to cellphone locational data, setting a precedent that could apply to cars.)

Another potential target is the pedestrian. In the first part of the 20th century, manufacturers lobbied to make "jaywalking" a crime, so the new horseless carriages could cruise along urban streets relatively unimpeded. The pedestrians of the future, emboldened by the fact that self-driving cars are sure to stop, could cause havoc. No worries, though: Facial-recognition technology is coming along nicely, and the automotive industry will be, if anything, even more powerful. Look for today's complaints about speeding tickets to be replaced by stories of "jaywalking traps" and pitiless fines for a second offense.

GARETH COOK IS A CONTRIBUTING WRITER FOR THE MAGAZINE. HIS LAST ARTICLE WAS ABOUT CANCER.

THE RISE AND FALL OF AQUACARS

BY JENNIFER KAHN

LOOKING BACK AT the decades when the autonomous car was developed, you may find it hard to believe that its engineers imagined that it would stay landbound. All along, sea levels continued to rise, gradually overwhelming the sea walls that many coastal cities built as protection and flooding the (now absurdly named) ground floor of apartment and office buildings.

Rather than simply abandon these buildings, though, many residents chose to stay — fueling a demand for autonomous aquacars and, as that technology improved, for mobile aquahomes. This became especially true after the successful completion of the SeaOrbiter, a floating laboratory originally designed for oceanography research. Elegant and semisubmersible, the SeaOrbiter acted as a kind of prototype for local offshore living — and the rise of aerial drone delivery, originally pioneered by Amazon, made the challenge of resupplying straightforward.

Unfortunately, hackers quickly figured out how to hijack the aquahomes' navigation system — first by disabling it and then with programs that directed vessels to floating "chop shops" run by roving gangs of ship-breakers. Piracy rates dropped only after huge kelp growth, driven by a mix of ocean warming and overfishing, rendered the submerged communities as unnavigable by aquacars as they had been by roadbound ones.

JENNIFER KAHN LAST WROTE FOR THE MAGAZINE ABOUT THE YOUTUBE SERIES "PRIMITIVE TECHNOLOGY."

THE END OF ROADKILL

BY MALIA WOLLAN

THE NEARLY 264 MILLION vehicles that people are driving over four million miles of American public roads these days add up to a kind of superspecies: a fast-moving predator that leaves its kill to rot on the side of the road. But once they are equipped with 360-degree-sensing technology that can see farther than the human eye and react more quickly, self-driving cars will — at least theoretically — have significant ecological impact. "If we don't kill animals with our vehicles anymore, are we willing to live with them in closer proximity to us?" says Patricia Cramer, a wildlife researcher who works with state transportation departments on roadkill issues. "Because that's what's going to happen."

The animals most imperiled by cars are top predators like the Florida panther. Vehicles are responsible for 59 percent of all known panther deaths recorded in the state since 1981; just last year, a record-breaking 34 panthers — about one-fourth of the estimated population — were killed on the state's roads. Most panthers are struck at night, when human vision is particularly poor, but long-distance infrared cameras can pick up a warmblooded feline body in the dark, far beyond the range of headlights. Panthers able to cross roads safely could spread out of the cramped confines of Florida's southern tip, move north into the Okefenokee Swamp and then farther into Georgia on their way to eventually repopulating the Southeast.

There is a concept in ecology called the trophic cascade, essentially the ripple effect on other animals when a top species vanishes. Over hundreds of years, humans methodically killed off predators like wolves, pumas and grizzly bears. Now, in many places, human drivers have become, albeit unintentionally, the top predator. Every year in the United States, there are an estimated 1.5 million deer-vehicle crashes. If self-driving cars manage to give deer safe passage, the fast-reproducing species would quickly grow beyond the ability of the vegetation to sustain them. "You'd get a lot of starvation and mass die-offs," says Daniel J. Smith, a conservation biologist at the University of Central Florida who has been studying road ecology for nearly three decades. Species like raccoons and Virginia opossums will most likely see population explosions. "There will be deer in people's yards, and there will be snipers in towns killing them," Cramer says.

This rewilding will be largely accidental, of course. Engineers will program cars to prioritize human life and property, making it far more likely they will stop for a moose than for a sparrow. Just how deferential they are toward wildlife will depend on human choices and ingenuity. For now, the heterogeneity and unpredictability of nature tends to confound the algorithms. In Australia, hopping kangaroos jumbled a self-driving Volvo's ability to measure distance. In Boston, autonomous-vehicle sensors identified a flock of sea gulls as a single form rather than a collection of individual birds. Still, even the tiniest creatures could benefit. "The car could know: 'O.K., this is a hot spot for frogs. It's spring. It's been raining. All the frogs will be moving across the road to find a mate,'" Smith says. The vehicles could reroute to avoid flattening amphibians on that critical day.

But for that to happen, the people making and buying the cars would need to regard them and the roads not just as a mode of transport but also as part of a vast and intricate ecological web. So far, most humans don't seem particularly inclined to this kind of systems thinking. It is more likely that a surge in animal populations will be just another unintended consequence of a technological shift — much like social-media sites becoming platforms for publishing fake news or, for that matter, the internal-combustion engine contributing to the suffocation of the planet that might eventually wipe out humans and animals alike. We tend to get caught, ill prepared, in storms of our own making. If one thing seems certain about the autonomous car, it's that we will go full speed ahead with it, even if we haven't entirely thought through the consequences.

MALIA WOLLAN IS THE TIP COLUMNIST FOR THE MAGAZINE.

Richard Branson's Virgin and Hyperloop One Transit Pods Become Fast Friends

BY JACEY FORTIN | OCT. 12, 2017

HIGH-SPEED HYPERLOOP TRANSIT — the futuristic concept involving passenger pods that could zip from, say, San Francisco to Los Angeles in a half-hour — just got a boost from Richard Branson.

The Virgin Group, the multinational venture capital corporation run by Mr. Branson, announced on Thursday that it was investing in Hyperloop One, a Los Angeles company that has been developing the transit technology since its founding in 2014.

Executives at Hyperloop One — now called Virgin Hyperloop One — and the Virgin Group would not reveal the size of the investment.

Nick Fox, the Virgin Group's chief communications officer, said Virgin did not become a majority shareholder in the young company, adding that Mr. Branson now has a seat on its board. He said the idea to invest came from Mr. Branson himself, who visited the site of a hyperloop test run in Nevada this year.

"Richard was excited by the concept," Mr. Fox said in a phone interview on Thursday. "He's always looking at the future of transport, whether it be in space or on land, and he's run trains for more than 20 years in the United Kingdom."

Virgin Group companies include Virgin Trains, a railroad operator in Britain, and Virgin Galactic, which is dedicated to commercial spaceflight.

Hyperloop One employees do not call their project a train — after all, it does not use tracks. Instead, magnetically levitating passenger pods use electric propulsion to zip through low-pressure tubes, transporting people and cargo at speeds of up to 670 miles per hour. That's the idea, at least: No human has taken one of these high-speed rides just yet.

DAVID BECKER/GETTY IMAGES

Sand rises from the track on May 2016, at the Hyperloop One Test and Safety site in North Las Vegas, as the company demonstrates a key component of its futuristic rail transit concept that could one day ferry passengers at near-supersonic speeds.

But Hyperloop One has been developing the technology for years, applying for dozens of patents and sending one pod on a successful 500-meter test run in July. Now the company is ramping up its business development and fund-raising.

"We would have done the branding deal and the partnership if they didn't invest a penny," Marvin Ammori, Hyperloop One's general counsel, said of Virgin in a phone interview on Thursday. "They have experience taking on incumbent industries with innovation."

The funding came during the company's last investment round, which closed in September and raised $85 million. In total, Hyperloop One has raised $245 million since 2014.

"This feels like the moment when all of this stuff is coming together," Mr. Ammori said.

High-speed travel in levitating pods is still in its early stages, so Hyperloop One is unable to say for sure when a working system might be in place — the target is 2021 — or where in the world that might be.

The company has reviewed thousands of proposals for routes in countries including Mexico, Britain, India and the United States, and it is testing the waters with governments around the world. "We consider it a race for the first hyperloop," Mr. Ammori said.

Hyperloop transit has its critics, who describe the idea as an ambitious pipe dream that has left many questions unanswered, including several about its cost. Some scoffed when Elon Musk, the serial tech entrepreneur, released a white paper on hyperloop technology in 2013 that claimed a link between San Francisco and Los Angeles could be completed for less than $6 billion. (More has been spent to renovate a single California bridge.)

Mr. Musk's white paper was made available to the public as means of encouraging hyperloop development. His own companies, which include SpaceX and Tesla, are not formally involved in Hyperloop One's work.

Why Even the Hyperloop Probably Wouldn't Change Your Commute Time

BY EMILY BADGER | AUG. 10, 2017

THE HYPERLOOP, Elon Musk has boasted, could whisk you from New York to Washington in 29 minutes. Other maglev boosters sell similar dreams: San Francisco to Los Angeles in under 30. Dallas to Houston, Portland to Seattle, Orlando to Miami in the same.

The half-hour trip is something of a mystical notion in transportation. These visions of the future sound seductive in part because half an hour is, in fact, roughly how long many of us spend getting to work. The typical American commutes 26.4 minutes, one way, according to the American Community Survey. Even in metro New York, with nearly the longest commutes in the country, that average is 36 minutes.

Of course plenty of workers trek less or much more, but average American commute times have budged only modestly over the last 35 years, since the census began asking about them. International studies have shown similar half-hour patterns. History even hints that the Romans traveled about the same, when most people went everywhere on foot.

The curious stability of the half-hour average commute means that when bullet trains — or autonomous vehicles, or whatever innovation comes next — link two places by that much time, they won't just open up plausible new weekend getaways and airline alternatives. They will also potentially restructure daily life: where people live, what jobs they hold, how cities expand over time.

"What Musk correctly realizes is that there will be a huge market with maglev or hyperloop technology for the places it connects in 30 minutes," said Jesse Ausubel, an environmental scientist at the Rockefeller University. "Any pairing that you can fit into that more or less one-hour round trip, the traffic will multiply immensely," he said, referring to the volume of travelers.

People priced out of Brooklyn could move to Baltimore. Congressional aides would commute to Philadelphia. Whole cities — and labor and housing markets — would fuse together.

The hyperloop is a wild hypothetical. But Mr. Ausubel's point stands on two related patterns from history. When you give people greater speed, they don't use it to save time; they use it to consume more space. As a result, cities have spread outward as transportation technology has evolved. Horse-drawn carriages enlarged pedestrian towns. Streetcars enabled streetcar suburbs. Highways made exurbia possible.

What, then, will cities look like with true high-speed rail, or autonomous cars, or even the hyperloop? What happens when 30 minutes of time buys you not two miles, or 10, but 200?

Transportation futurists partly anticipate this question (if not all the ripple effects their innovations will bring): "We're not selling transportation," the company Hyperloop One says. "We're selling time."

And time, in transportation, means territory.

The accompanying maps illustrate how that territory changes as the means of travel does. Starting at the 30th Street Station in Philadelphia, a city once crossable on foot, the transportation analysis consultancy Conveyal plotted for us how far a person can travel in 30 minutes by foot, by transit and by car today. We then made some predictions about what the future of high-speed rail and autonomous cars could look like for the same commuter setting out in the middle of the Northeast corridor.

The law of the 30-minute commute is known as Marchetti's constant, named for the Italian physicist Cesare Marchetti, a mentor to Mr. Ausubel. Mr. Marchetti picked up the work of Yacov Zahavi, a transportation engineer who theorized in the 1970s and '80s that people have a fixed travel-time budget. We allocate part of our day to getting around. And that amount, about an hour, Mr. Zahavi argued, holds steady no matter where we live or how we travel.

Mr. Marchetti noted supporting historical clues: Ancient Rome, Persepolis and Marrakesh were about five kilometers across, or the maximum distance most people can travel in an hour on foot. He diagramed the growth of Berlin, which appeared to expand concentrically as transportation advances enlarged the land people could cover. He found it not coincidental that modern-day prisons still allow inmates one humane concession — the freedom to pace for an hour outdoors.

"From our anthropological point of view, humans are territorial animals," said Mr. Ausubel, who wrote numerous papers with Mr. Marchetti on the topic. "So they seek to maximize range, which equates with resources. And those resources can be jobs or education, or fields for rice or wheat, or social life."

We're hard-wired to roam farther, they argue, when more speed allows us to. (By this same theory, delays in the New York subway disturb something deeply embedded in the human mind.)

Researchers today are not universally sold on Marchetti's constant. Some developing-world cities have monstrous commutes. Alex Anas, an economist who has modeled the future growth of cities like Chicago, finds that commute times stay relatively stable even as population and developed land area grow. But that's because the distribution of jobs and the behavior of workers shift in response to congestion, he says. It's not because humans have some innate hourlong travel budget. "Economists don't buy that," Mr. Anas said.

But part of what Mr. Marchetti described is proved by history.

"In the past, when you put in new transportation lines, cities grew further away — we know that is a fact, with or without Marchetti," said Carlo Ratti, director of the Senseable City Lab at M.I.T., which has tried to validate Mr. Marchetti's theories using commuters' cellphone data.

In the future, superfast trains will put a twist on this picture.

"What we're going to see with some of these new proposals is not necessarily that cities will grow much bigger," Mr. Ratti said. "But we're going to see two cities become one, in terms of culture, in terms of the labor market, in terms of universities."

Philadelphia and Washington could become linked the way Manhattan and Brooklyn are today, if the travel costs are comparable (recall, before approval of the New York subway, that the boroughs were separate cities). High-speed rail in parts of Europe and Japan has already begun to have such effects.

Such an agglomeration then has all kinds of implications.

Luis Bettencourt, who heads the Mansueto Institute for Urban Innovation at the University of Chicago, said cities could start to specialize even more than they do today. "It could be that you have to go to Boston for surgery, and New York for the arts, and Philadelphia for something else," he said.

In the Northeast corridor, we don't quite need hyperloop-level speeds to get there. Conveyal modeled a high-speed rail line, similar in route to the Acela, that reaches 300 miles an hour. That's a little faster than the fastest operating speed for a train in the world today, the Shanghai maglev. With direct service, it would take you from Philadelphia to Wilmington, Del., in 10 minutes, to Newark in 18, to New York's Penn Station in 21 and to Washington's Union Station in 29.

A rail line that fast would effectively link the two city centers as if they were no farther apart than Times Square and the Barclays Center.

Autonomous vehicles have a murkier future. They could support denser cities by eliminating parking spaces and enabling efficient ride-sharing. Or they could create even more sprawl. They may give commuters greater speed — even without higher speed limits — by reducing congestion and car wrecks, or with vehicle platooning and synchronized traffic lights. (In our predictions, we assume that mass adoption of autonomous cars could mean travel that is about 33 percent faster.)

That picture, though, depends on whether autonomous vehicles make up the entire market, or just part of it. And they could wholly upend Mr. Marchetti's theories: If a car becomes a traveling office, will people even mentally measure their commutes as "travel time"?

Mr. Marchetti fantasized about the future long before Mr. Musk did.

He and Mr. Ausubel even developed ideas for maglevs that traveled in low-pressure tubes. Before today's hyperloop slogans, Mr. Marchetti mused about Casablanca-to-Paris in just 20 minutes.

"In other words," he wrote, "a woman in Casablanca could go to work in Paris, and cook dinner for her children in the evening."

Whether that idea thrills or alarms you is another question.

Falcon Heavy, in a Roar of Thunder, Carries SpaceX's Ambition Into Orbit

BY KENNETH CHANG | FEB. 6, 2018

Elon Musk disrupted the business of sending rockets into space and has now achieved a milestone by launching the most powerful rocket currently operating.

KENNEDY SPACE CENTER, FLA. — From the same pad where NASA launched rockets that carried astronauts to the moon, a big, new American rocket arced into space on Tuesday. But this time, NASA was not involved. The rocket, the Falcon Heavy, was built by SpaceX, the company founded and run by the billionaire entrepreneur Elon Musk.

"It seems surreal to me," Mr. Musk said during a news conference after the launch.

The launch of this turbocharged version of the workhorse Falcon 9 rocket, which has been carrying cargo to space for years, marks an important milestone in spaceflight, the first time a rocket this powerful has been sent into space by a private company rather than a government space agency.

The rocket carried a playful payload: Mr. Musk's red Roadster, an electric sports car built by his other company, Tesla. Strapped inside the car is a mannequin wearing one of SpaceX's spacesuits. They are expected to orbit the sun for hundreds of millions of years.

The success gives SpaceX momentum to begin developing even larger rockets, which could help fulfill Mr. Musk's dream of sending people to Mars. To do that, he has described a new-generation rocket called B.F.R. (the B stands for big; the R for rocket) that might be ready to launch in the mid-2020s.

The near-flawless performance of the Heavy on Tuesday "gives me a lot of confidence we can make the B.F.R. design work," Mr. Musk said.

He added that he hoped the launch would encourage other companies and other countries to aim for more ambitious goals in space.

TODD ANDERSON FOR THE NEW YORK TIMES

Elon Musk, the founder of SpaceX, at Launch Pad 39A at the Kennedy Space Center in Florida, where the Falcon Heavy rocket launched.

"We want a new space race," he said. "Races are exciting."

Mr. Musk's visions include humans living both on Earth and Mars. He's part of a new generation of entrepreneurial space pioneers that includes Jeffrey P. Bezos, the founder of Amazon, who has said one of the goals driving his rocket company, Blue Origin, is the prospect of millions of people living in space. Planetary Resources, an American company with a large investment from Luxembourg, hopes to mine asteroids for profit. Moon Express, based in Florida, sees a business in providing regular transportation to and from the moon.

For now, the Heavy will enable SpaceX to compete for contracts to launch larger spy satellites, and some experts in spaceflight are encouraging NASA to use private rockets like the Heavy instead of the gigantic and more expensive rocket, the Space Launch System, that is currently being developed in part to take astronauts back to the moon.

"It basically gives them another tool in their toolbox for accomplishing the space community's goals," said Phil Larson, an assistant dean at the University of Colorado's engineering school who previously worked as a senior manager of communications and corporate projects at SpaceX.

Although delayed by high-altitude winds, the countdown proceeded smoothly, without any of the glitches that have bedeviled other maiden launches of new rockets.

The Heavy roared to life, a plume of smoke and steam shooting sideways from the launchpad. It rose from the pad, with an impossibly bright glare of 27 engines beneath it.

About 15 seconds later, a thunderous roar, traveling at the speed of sound, rolled over the spectators.

Just over three minutes after it blasted off, the most suspenseful part of the flight was over, as the boosters dropped off and the second stage continued into Earth orbit.

Some eight minutes after launch, a pair of sonic booms rocked the area as the two side boosters set down in near synchrony on two landing pads at Cape Canaveral. In the past few years, SpaceX has figured out how to routinely bring a booster stage back in one piece to fly again on future flights.

The one blemish on the mission was that the center booster, which was to set down on a floating platform in the Atlantic, slammed into the water instead, because some of the engines failed to ignite for the final landing burn.

Once in orbit, the rocket sent back video of the spacesuit-wearing mannequin in the car, with a hand on the steering wheel. On the dashboard were the words "Don't Panic," a nod to Douglas Adams's book "The Hitchhiker's Guide to the Galaxy."

The spacecraft journeyed through Earth's Van Allen radiation belt. About seven hours after the rocket took off, Mr. Musk announced that a third and final burn had put his sports car on an elliptical orbit away from Earth and around the sun that extends beyond Mars's orbit.

Since 2010, the company has been sending the smaller Falcon 9 rocket into orbit, deploying satellites and carrying cargo to crews aboard the International Space Station. The company has disrupted the global launch business with its lower prices and reusable boosters.

The Falcon Heavy is capable of lifting 140,000 pounds to low-Earth orbit, more than any other rocket today. Because all three boosters are to be recovered to fly again, a Falcon Heavy launch costs not much more than one by the company's existing rocket, Mr. Musk said. SpaceX lists a price of $90 million for a Falcon Heavy flight, compared with $62 million for one by Falcon 9, a bargain in the context of spaceflight.

Mr. Musk estimated that his company had spent more than half a billion dollars on Falcon Heavy and said that the program was almost canceled three times.

SpaceX has booked coming Heavy flights for Arabsat, a Saudi Arabian communications company, and the United States Air Force.

However, the market for the Heavy is smaller than what Mr. Musk envisioned when he announced development of the rocket in 2011. Back then, he expected that SpaceX's launches would be evenly split between Falcon 9s and Heavies.

JIM WATSON/AFP/GETTY IMAGES

Two of the Falcon Heavy's boosters returning to Earth at Cape Canaveral eight minutes after launch.

But the development of the Heavy took years longer than anticipated — the central booster had to be redesigned to withstand the stresses of the powerful side boosters — and with advances in miniaturization, the trend is toward smaller satellites. SpaceX also boosted the capability of the Falcon 9, which now can launch many of the payloads that would have originally required a Heavy.

In addition to its central booster, the Falcon Heavy was equipped with two additional side boosters that essentially tripled its power at liftoff. While the Heavy uses many of the same components as the Falcon 9, Mr. Musk had cautioned that failures during a test flight would not be surprising. In particular, he worried about complex buffeting of air flowing past the boosters, which is difficult to predict even with the most sophisticated computer simulations.

The success of the Heavy could quell criticism that followed SpaceX's first launch of the year — a Falcon 9 rocket that carried a highly classified payload code-named "Zuma," on Jan. 7. A day after the launch, there were reports that Zuma had fallen back to Earth. SpaceX officials vociferously asserted that the Falcon 9 performed as expected, suggesting that blame for anything that went wrong should fall on Northrop Grumman, which built Zuma.

In the past year, SpaceX has tabled many of the plans for future development of the Heavy. The company had intended to use the rocket to launch one of SpaceX's capsules, known as the Dragon, without people, on a mission to land on Mars. That was scrapped last summer.

Last year, Mr. Musk also said two space tourists would be launched by a Falcon Heavy on an around-the-moon trip this year. On Monday, he said that for now the company had no immediate plans to make the improvements needed before putting people aboard.

Instead, SpaceX is focusing its efforts on the B.F.R. It would be a two-stage rocket: a powerful booster to provide lift out of Earth's gravity and then a spaceship on top for interplanetary missions. The full vehicle would not be ready until the 2020s, but Mr. Musk said he had "aspirational" hopes to begin short hopper tests of the spaceship portion next year.

CHAPTER 3

Blockchain and Cryptocurrencies

Cryptocurrency, a decentralized digital form of currency, is not controlled or managed by any one government, company or person. Bitcoin was the first cryptocurrency. What made it different from previous digital cash systems was blockchain technology. Blockchain — a continuously growing list of records, or blocks, that are linked and secured using cryptography — was developed by the creator of bitcoin. It allowed spenders and receivers of bitcoin to record every use, creating a network of trust between users. Innovators are now adapting blockchain for use in other markets, such as real estate and energy production.

Speed Bumps on the Road to Virtual Cash

BY NOAM COHEN | JULY 3, 2011

MONEY IS ACCUMULATED, traded and transferred online every day, but can there be a form of currency that exists only online and yet has real-world value?

That is the premise of Bitcoin, an open-source virtual currency system that since 2009 has grown to a market worth more than $100 million.

But the past few weeks have shown that a virtual currency can be just as vulnerable as the paper kind. Bitcoin accounts have been subject to hacking and theft; the currency itself experienced a bubble and a crash. And at least one group that was collecting donations in Bitcoins has decided against using them because of possible legal entanglements.

Gavin Andresen, who is the lead developer of the open-source software that operates the currency, said in an interview from his home in Amherst, Mass.: "I expected it to have lots of speed bumps along the way — but I didn't expect there to be so many speed bumps in a row."

There are several appeals to the idea of an online currency. The standard way to ensure the validity of online transactions, according to Jerry Brito, a technology expert at George Mason University, is "to have an intermediary to keep the ledger," that is, a service like PayPal or a credit card company that takes a percentage of the transaction.

A virtual currency would not need an intermediary. It would also make it harder for authorities to track transactions (particularly appealing for gambling sites or other quasi-legal activities).

Bitcoin began as a kind of thought experiment. In 2009, an anonymous programmer published a paper proposing a virtual currency that would elegantly solve many of the problems surrounding currency that exists only on the Internet, including the main one, that the money would simply be copied like, say, music files, and plummet in value.

Another part of the challenge was to create a currency without having to resort to a central bank to issue the currency and track the transactions. In other words, the transactions would be genuinely "peer-to-peer" rather than pass though a virtual bank.

The solution of the Bitcoin programmer, who wrote under the name Satoshi Nakamoto, was to ensure that each "coin" was its own certificate of authenticity — that the coin, in essence, would be nothing more than that certificate.

In the Bitcoin system, a new coin is produced whenever a computer can calculate an answer to a difficult problem, and then attaches that answer to a digital record of every transaction of every Bitcoin ever traded — a breathtakingly large amount of information to carry around in order to buy a pack of gum, but in a time when information can zip around the Internet, not too much to ask. Anyone would be free to create a new coin, within proscribed supply limits, by having a computer do the work needed to prove that it was in fact a valid Bitcoin.

"The incentives are right, they are a check that everyone is following the rules," said Mr. Andresen. "Early adopters want it to succeed, because they already own the currency. And if you generate Bitcoins no one thinks is valid, you have wasted a lot of computer time."

In fact, Bitcoin is a rarity for a currency in that it is neither a so-called fiat currency — one like dollars, which are valuable because the government says they are — nor is it a specie currency, one that gets its value because it can be converted into a precious metal like silver or gold.

But why would a Bitcoin have value if it is only a stream of numbers, unsupported by government fiat or by some underlying asset?

"Why does any tool have value?" Mr. Andresen asked. "It is valuable because it is useful."

Starting almost as soon as the coins were introduced, they have been traded for dollars at online exchanges, serving as a crude measure of the currency's popularity and health (and also giving a market where owners can trade in Bitcoins for real dollars).

After two years, there are seven million of these "coins" in circulation and the rate of increase — currently 50 coins are added every 10 minutes — will slow each year until the number tops out at 21 million coins around 2025. The coins, which trade for about $17 each at online exchanges, have a cumulative value of about $100 million. "I do think of it as the market cap of Bitcoin," said Mr. Andresen. Today, a list of businesses that accept Bitcoin currency is a motley collection of companies on the fringe of the computer world, groups that conduct gambling or the like, and, notably, the antisecrecy group WikiLeaks, which accepts contributions in Bitcoins. You certainly can't stock the pantry or furnish your home with Bitcoins.

When reached by phone, a bookstore owner on the list, Sonny Saul, from Woodstock, Vt., said that he had had the account for only a week and a half and that he had "no practical experience with it yet, other than your phone call."

Mr. Saul said his son was a fan of Bitcoins and had set up an account for him; he said he was intrigued.

"I might be able to bypass Visa and Mastercard — they take 2 to 3 percent on every transaction," he said, adding that if it "eliminates the need for a central bank — I am interested philosophically how it would affect society."

A Hungarian woman, Judit Whelan, 33, who sells pet accessories at the Critter Casual and was persuaded to accept the coins by her husband, a computer programmer, said that she had more success.

"I've sold 24 collars, 13 leashes and 1 pair of 'Disco Knickers' with Bitcoin over the last few months," she wrote in an e-mail. "The first order I had was for 42 BTC, which was worth about $40 at the time, but now those coins would be worth around $680! Originally I had a fixed Bitcoin price, but now I do a conversion based on the exchange rate."

But the currency proved to be so unstable, Mr. Andresen said, that it became hard to use as a "unit of account." When they began, they were worth fractions of a penny. They rose to more than $30, a market cap of more than $210 million, and now trade roughly in the middle.

And the system has had to weather other challenges. In June alone, there have been thefts of virtual wallets that have been left unprotected on Bitcoin owners' hard drives; the biggest case was said to involve coins with a trading value of $500,000.

Similarly, security firms say they have detected "bots" that hijack unsuspecting computers to do the calculating necessary to create new coins on other peoples' dime.

Even more spectacularly, the largest trader of Bitcoins, the Mt.Gox exchange, said it was hacked on June 19, with certain accounts being emptied and others being used to trade imaginary Bitcoins and, in the process, drop the value of Bitcoins to pennies.

In a coincidence of timing, the Electronic Frontier Foundation, an Internet rights advocacy group in San Francisco, announced that it would not be accepting the Bitcoins that had been donated via an account in its name, in order to avoid any legal entanglements with the service.

The group would be returning coins that at one time were worth $100,000 to the Bitcoin community because of the uncertain legal picture, its legal director, Cindy Cohn said. “We didn’t want to be a participant in this,” she said.

Mr. Andresen said he imagined that after the bubbles, the currency would find enthusiasts, beyond the traders: “Anything that is purely in the electronic world,” he said. “Digital downloads, Web hosting, programming services — especially if it is international — those would be the early niches.”

Mr. Brito was optimistic about Bitcoins finding consistent users. But as with many online innovations, the early adopters tend to occupy a different, if marginal, niche.

“This is a censorship-proof currency that allows transactions to happen,” he said. “Right now what are those sort of transactions? Gambling, buying drugs — that is what is going to jumpstart it.”

Bubble or No, This Virtual Currency Is a Lot of Coin in Any Realm

BY NOAM COHEN | APRIL 7, 2013

WHEN HE WAS a Yale Law School student, Reuben Grinberg wrote one of the first academic papers about Bitcoin, a novel virtual currency that uses sophisticated cryptography to validate and secure transactions that exist only online.

When Mr. Grinberg, now a lawyer in the financial institutions group of the Manhattan law firm Davis Polk & Wardwell, first learned about bitcoins, they were selling for 10 cents. Now, after the latest price surge that began in January, the cost of a bitcoin on an exchange that converts them to dollars is something like $140, and the collective value of all bitcoins has passed a billion dollars.

That is a lot of coin in any form, and the billion-dollar milestone has turned the once-obscure online currency into a media sensation. Had Mr. Grinberg invested just $100 back then, today his investment would be worth ...

Ah, but that way madness lies. "People are buying bitcoins because the price is going up," he said in an interview. "That is the classic indicator of a bubble."

The question of whether the increase represents real value or is simply evidence of a bubble is at the heart of the current media frenzy. Bitcoin began in January 2009, a project introduced by a programmer or group of programmers who worked under the name Satoshi Nakamoto.

The project represented a breakthrough in using software code to authenticate and protect transactions without resorting to a centralized bank or government treasury. In that way, Bitcoin became a peer-to-peer system. That comes in pretty handy for people who do not want their transactions monitored.

In conversations about the project with scholars who study it, the word that comes up as often as "bubble" is "genius."

For one thing, though bitcoins are software code, you can't simply copy them like a music file. The process of creating the coins — "mining" them in the project's allusion to something tangible like gold or silver — involves computer work that, crucially, verifies Bitcoin transactions.

"It is the most successful digital currency already right now," said Nicolas Christin, the associate director of the Information Networking Institute at Carnegie Mellon University. "Even if bitcoins become worth nothing, it has succeeded more than any academic proposals for a digital currency," he said in an interview from Okinawa, Japan, where he was attending a conference on financial cryptography that included a number of papers on bitcoins.

People buy the coins for cold hard cash on exchanges. Completing those purchases, as well as cashing out, typically involves re-entering the world of traditional financial transactions, with fees and loss of anonymity.

But Bitcoin's managers say the currency has proved so secure that despite the fact that exchanges and virtual wallets, where people keep their bitcoins, have been hacked, the coins themselves have not been forged.

So why the sudden run-up in value? Some point to the recent crisis over Cypriot banks, which made a currency beyond the control of governments more tempting. And as with a run-up in anything tradable — tulip bulbs, dot-com shares — there is also the hypnotic logic that says the price went up today, so that means it will go up tomorrow.

Some observers and investors also make the case that bitcoins are in fact undervalued. Their argument goes like this. The total value of the world's economic activity is enormous. There are certain transactions that are ideal for bitcoins because the currency is relatively anonymous and does not need to be processed by a financial organization or a government.

NANCY PALMIERI FOR THE NEW YORK TIMES

Bitbills are physical representations of the virtual currency known as bitcoins.

If bitcoins become the dominant currency in some small niche of the world economy — that is, those people who do not want their transactions easily tracked or who want to send money back home from abroad — then they will become quite valuable indeed. This outcome has been neatly summarized by the financial blogger Felix Salmon as making bitcoins an "uncomfortable combination of commodity and currency."

The price increase becomes a question of supply and demand. Unlike other currencies that can adjust the money supply depending on economic conditions, bitcoins have a supply that is fixed. The amount of new coins that can be minted was plotted at the outset with a finite number of coins at the end, roughly 21 million in the next century. Today, the rate is 25 new coins every 10 minutes; for the first four years, it was twice as many, 50 every 10 minutes.

The slowdown in the rate new coins are added, which was programmed into bitcoins, may also help account for the spike in prices.

So far, excluding investors and day traders, the main use of the currency appears to be illicit activity. There are the online gambling sites that use bitcoins. And the anonymous online marketplace Silk Road, which accepts only bitcoins, is "overwhelmingly used as a market for controlled substances and narcotics," according to a paper on Silk Road written by Mr. Christin of Carnegie Mellon.

He used clues on the site, including buyer feedback reports, to calculate how much and what kind of business was being transacted. His conclusion, as of July 2012, was that $1.2 million in business was carried out each month, much of it for buying small amounts of narcotics that were delivered by mail. "We did see it was growing," he said of the total value of the trades. "It pretty much doubled in the six months I followed it."

Excluding the traders, he said, "Silk Road probably represents a sizable amount of bitcoin exchanges, but not more than half."

Supporters of the Bitcoin project acknowledge these statistics but argue that it can still thrive as a mainstream currency.

"I think when you talk about Silk Road, you are talking about the first early adopter market — there is no other solution that works," said Gavin Andresen, chief scientist at the Bitcoin Foundation, a nonprofit organization that manages the project. When the currency evolves to be more useful and better known, he said, it will be used for more mundane transactions.

Even the idea that it is experiencing a bubble — and Mr. Andresen said in an interview by phone from Amherst, Mass., "I think it definitely is a frenzy" — is for the best. "Eventually the media gets bored and moves on to the next thing," he said, "and what is left behind is a whole new wave of people interested." And, he says, a much lower price for bitcoins.

As evidence of mainstream interest, Mr. Andresen pointed to the Bitcoin 2013 conference in San Jose, Calif., next month, which is attracting entrepreneurs with Silicon Valley venture capital backing. The list of panelists is heavy with start-up executives, but includes some activists — including representatives from the Web site Antiwar.com and the Electronic Frontier Foundation — who see a currency outside of government regulation as crucial to financing projects that criticize the authorities.

Mr. Andresen is not a mere bystander to the fluctuations in bitcoin prices. As an employee of the Bitcoin Foundation, after working as volunteer on the software, he is paid in bitcoins, with the rate set every three months. In 2013, his salary in terms of dollars has increased more than tenfold.

Starting in April, however, the foundation has decided that, because of those fluctuations, his bitcoin salary would be adjusted each month, he said. Still, that alone makes this bubble different than many in the past: the creators are not looking to get their money and make a quick exit.

What Is Bitcoin, and How Does It Work?

BY NATHANIEL POPPER | OCT. 1, 2017

IF YOU FIND the concept of Bitcoin confusing, you are not alone. The virtual currency has been a constant source of controversy, but it is still not well understood.

Currently, the average price of one Bitcoin is about $7,629, according to Blockchain.info, a news and data site.

ARE BITCOINS THOSE COINS I SEE IN PHOTOGRAPHS?

No. Those coins are novelty items that newspapers used in photographs because they couldn't find anything else to illustrate their stories about Bitcoin.

A Bitcoin is a digital token — with no physical backing — that can be sent electronically from one user to another, anywhere in the world. A Bitcoin can be divided out to eight decimal places, so you can send someone 0.00000001 Bitcoins. This smallest fraction of a Bitcoin — the penny of the Bitcoin world — is referred to as a Satoshi, after the anonymous creator of Bitcoin.

This all gets confusing, because Bitcoin is also the name of the payment network on which the Bitcoin digital tokens are stored and moved.

Unlike traditional payment networks like Visa, the Bitcoin network is not run by a single company or person. The system is run by a decentralized network of computers around the world that keep track of all Bitcoin transactions, similar to the way Wikipedia is maintained by a decentralized network of writers and editors.

The record of all Bitcoin transactions that these computers are constantly updating is known as the blockchain.

WHY DO CRIMINALS LIKE BITCOIN?

Criminals have taken to Bitcoin because anyone can open a Bitcoin address and start sending and receiving Bitcoins without giving a name or identity. There is no central authority that could collect this information.

Bitcoin first took off in 2011 after drug dealers began taking payments in Bitcoin on the black-market website known as the Silk Road. Although the Silk Road was shut down in 2013, similar sites have popped up to replace it.

More recently, Bitcoin has become a method for making ransom payments — for example, when your computer is taken over by so-called ransomware.

WHY WON'T THE GOVERNMENT JUST SHUT IT DOWN?

The records of the Bitcoin network, including all balances and transactions, are stored on every computer helping to maintain the network — about 9,500 computers in late 2017.

If the government made it illegal for Americans to participate in this network, the computers and people keeping the records in other countries would still be able to continue. The decentralized nature of Bitcoin is also one of the qualities that have made it popular with people who are suspicious of government authorities.

CAN BITCOIN USERS GIVE THEMSELVES MORE BITCOINS?

Anyone helping to maintain the database of all Bitcoin transactions — the blockchain — could change his or her own copy of the records to add more money. But if someone did that, the other computers maintaining the records would see the discrepancy, and the changes would be ignored.

ARE THERE LEGAL USES?

Only a small percentage of all transactions on the Bitcoin network are explicitly illegal. Most transactions are people buying and selling Bitcoins on exchanges, speculating on future prices. A whole world of high-frequency traders has sprung up around Bitcoin.

DANNY GHITIS FOR THE NEW YORK TIMES

A Bitcoin A.T.M. in the Hell's Kitchen neighborhood of Manhattan.

People in countries with high inflation, like Argentina and Venezuela, have bought Bitcoin with their local currency to avoid losing their savings to inflation.

One of the most popular business plans is to use Bitcoin to move money over international borders. Large international money transfers can take weeks when they go through banks, while millions of dollars of Bitcoin can be moved in minutes. So far, though, these practical applications of Bitcoin have been slow to take off.

HOW CAN I BUY A BITCOIN?

There are companies in most countries that will sell you Bitcoins in exchange for the local currency. In the United States, a company called Coinbase will link to your bank account or credit card and then sell you the coins for dollars. Opening an account with Coinbase is similar to opening a traditional bank or stock brokerage account, with lots of identity verification to satisfy the authorities.

For people who do not want to reveal their identities, services like LocalBitcoins will connect people who want to meet in person to buy and sell Bitcoins for cash, generally without any verification of identity required.

WHO DECIDES WHAT A BITCOIN IS WORTH?

The price of Bitcoin fluctuates constantly and is determined by open-market bidding on Bitcoin exchanges, similar to the way that stock and gold prices are determined by bidding on exchanges.

WHAT IS BITCOIN MINING?

Bitcoin mining refers to the process through which new Bitcoins are created and given to computers helping to maintain the network. The computers involved in Bitcoin mining are in a sort of computational race to process new transactions coming onto the network. The winner — generally the person with the fastest computers — gets a chunk of new Bitcoins, 12.5 of them right now. (The reward is halved every four years.)

There is generally a new winner about every 10 minutes, and there will be until there are 21 million Bitcoins in the world. At that point, no new Bitcoins will be created. This cap is expected to be reached in 2140. So far, about 16 million Bitcoin have been distributed.

Every Bitcoin in existence was created through this method and initially given to a computer helping to maintain the records. Anyone can set his or her computer to mine Bitcoin, but these days only people with specialized hardware manage to win the race.

ARE THERE BITCOIN COMPETITORS?

Plenty. But these other virtual currencies do not have as many followers as Bitcoin, so they are not worth as much. As in the real world, a currency is worth only as much as the number of people willing to accept it for goods and services.

JONATHAN ALCORN/BLOOMBERG VIA GETTY IMAGES

The man who some claimed was the Bitcoin founder, Satoshi Nakamoto, arriving at his home in Temple City, Calif., in 2014.

WHO IS SATOSHI NAKAMOTO?

Bitcoin was introduced in 2008 by an unknown creator going by the name of Satoshi Nakamoto, who communicated only by email and social messaging. While several people have been identified as likely candidates to be Satoshi, as the creator is known in the world of Bitcoin, no one has been confirmed as the real Satoshi, and the search has gone on.

Satoshi created the original rules of the Bitcoin network and then released the software to the world in 2009. Satoshi largely disappeared from view two years later. Anyone can download and use the software, and Satoshi now has no more control over the network than anyone else using the software.

Grandpa Had a Pension. This Generation Has Cryptocurrency.

BY TEDDY WAYNE | AUG. 3, 2017

MOST READERS HAVE probably heard of Bitcoin, the digital coin that dominates the cryptocurrency market. It has gained notice both because of its skyrocketing value (from less than a cent in early 2010 to around $2,600 currently) and because it is frequently a key player in hacking- and black-market-related stories, from the looting of nearly half a billion dollars in coins from the Mt. Gox exchange in 2014 to the recent demand for payment in Bitcoin in the WannaCry ransomware attack. (For the uninitiated, here is a useful primer on Bitcoin.)

But do you know Ethereum, with a total value of coins in circulation of close to $20 billion? Bitcoin Cash, which split off from the original Bitcoin on Aug. 1, lost about half its value within hours, then nearly quadrupled by the next day? Or, rounding out the Big Four, Ripple — whose currency is known as XRP — which shot up to about 40 cents by mid-May from less than a cent at the end of March? (Full disclosure: I owned but unloaded three of these currencies before writing this article.) Then there are over 800 lower-value and often creatively named coins among those listed on Coinmarketcap.com. One can buy FedoraCoin (its jaunty symbol being the Justin Timberlake-approved hat), CannabisCoin (one guess what it looks like) or, to choose one of many bringing up the rear, Quartz, currently priced around three-thousandths of a cent. (Bad news for those who bought it at just under $2 at the end of May.)

After years as a niche market for technologically sophisticated anarchists and libertarians excited about a decentralized financial network not under government control, digital coins may be on the verge of going mainstream. "It's the wild, wild West," said Ron Ginn, 35, founder of a private photo-sharing service called Text Event Pics in St. Augustine, Fla., who has taken all his money out of the stock market

JAMES HEIMER

and put it into Ripple and real estate. “This is like getting to invest in the internet in the ’90s. I’m obviously very bullish, but I expect to make a couple million dollars off very little money. This is the opportunity of a lifetime. Finance is getting its internet.”

Cryptocurrency has understandable appeal to millennials who came of age during the 2008 financial crisis and are now watching the rise of antiglobalist populism threaten the stability of the international economy.

“There’s a low cost for entry, you don’t pay a lot of fees and millennials are the most tech-savvy,” said John Guarco, 22, a recent Duke graduate living on Staten Island who, like most of the people interviewed for this article, asked that names of the coins in which he has invested not be published for fear of being targeted by hackers.

Unlike previous generations, many of these greenhorn investors don’t have pensions or 401(k)s, are mistrustful of socking money away in mutual funds and are fully accustomed to owning digital assets that have no concrete properties. As traditional paths to upper-middle-class stability are being blocked by debt, exorbitant housing costs and a shaky job market, these investors view cryptocurrency not only as a hedge against another Dow Jones crash, but also as the most rational — and even utopian — means of investing their money.

Sebastian Dinges, 33, the director of operations for Cheeky, a company that makes mealtime products, started his first job after college in 2007. Once he had enough money to invest in the stock market, he said, he "wanted to be risky and get a big return." Within six months, the market crashed.

"So there's definitely disillusionment," he said.

The majority of Mr. Dinges's holdings are now in cryptocurrency. His skepticism of traditional markets is shared by a number of cryptocurrency enthusiasts in his age bracket who have observed the recent political and economic upheavals.

"I do feel we've reached a new level where nobody knows what's going to happen," said Gabe Wax, 24, who runs the Rare Book Room recording studio in Brooklyn. "The things we've been able to rely on aren't as reliable and we have a president who knows absolutely nothing about how the economy works, and he's appointed people who have twisted views about how it works. That, more than anything, is what scares me."

Mr. Wax was still in high school when the 2008 crisis unfolded, but he was paying attention to the headlines. So was Mr. Guarco, who said cryptocurrency was a "safeguard against the volatility in the rest of the world."

"Investing in cryptocurrencies is a hedge," he continued. "We're entering a period of long-term deregulation and tax cuts to the wealthiest. It's not the best recipe for stability."

Mr. Wax also invests in cryptocurrency to shore up his finances as a freelancer in the precarious music industry.

"I constantly feel like I'm looking over the edge of a cliff," he said. "I don't like the idea of money just sitting in a savings account — with the way inflation works and how low interest rates are, you're losing money.

There's less money than there's ever been in the history of recorded music, so that gives me anxiety. It's weird to say that owning cryptocurrency soothes that anxiety, because it's counterintuitive, but it does."

He is far from the only one hoping cryptocurrency will assuage his financial worries. Internet forums and Twitter accounts devoted to the subject abound with speculators who view digital coins as a lottery ticket, forecasting "moonshots" with, perhaps, irrational exuberance. For office drudges, the underemployed or those crushed by college loans, the slim chance that a $100 investment may someday reap close to $100 million — as would have happened with an investment of that amount in Bitcoin in 2010 — is too enticing to pass up.

But there are plenty of dissenters who are less sanguine about the future of cryptocurrency, arguing that we are in the midst of the biggest bubble yet, fueled by speculative trading in Japan and South Korea, and pointing to previous Bitcoin crashes as justification for their skepticism.

Nevertheless, it's not just twentysomethings in the gig economy who are losing faith in traditional investment tools. Mr. Ginn quit working at Fidelity Investments the day before the market crash in 2008.

"It's not investing," he said of his old job. "It's just sticking money somewhere. The investment advisory industry has to give out watered-down, averaged-out advice. When you get into mutual funds, you lose a lot of the ability to beat the markets."

Tom Berg, 44, a founder of BloKtek Capital in Northbrook, Ill., which invests in digital currencies and assets, said: "I got out of the stock market years ago. "My personal opinion was I'm not going to fight for 2 or 3 percent. It's a conservative place." By contrast, digital currencies — his preferred term to cryptocurrency, which he says carries the stigma of black-market money laundering — have disrupted the internet and created a major opportunity for those willing to jump in early, Mr. Berg believes. "At first it was an internet of information," he said. "Then it evolved to an internet of things — social media, I can buy this, I can sell stuff. Now it's the internet of value."

In his view, cryptocurrency left the "dark ages" six months ago, when it was still the domain of "a lot of people who believed in anarchy." He thinks that cryptocurrency is a good five years from going mainstream and that the bubble will burst some time after that, at which point he will sell his assets.

"If my landscaper ever asks me about crypto, that's the day I get out," he said.

There are some barriers to mass popularity. Investors must have enough familiarity with and trust of the internet to send money through a cryptocurrency exchange, such as Coinbase or Poloniex. Some of the exchanges also have elaborate and slow identity-verification processes, and certain states do not permit users to invest on them yet. But it's continually getting easier, and various exchanges allow credit cards for speedy purchases.

Once one has bought digital coins, the threat of hacking remains a serious concern. Even users savvy enough to use two-factor authentication on their phones may not have the know-how to set up "cold storage," or a system of storing coins offline (such as on a computer or dedicated piece of hardware not connected to the internet). There is no Federal Deposit Insurance Corporation insuring lost money; once it's gone, it's gone.

Assuming one's money is protected, there are, of course, the standard risks of investing, amplified by the volatility of cryptocurrency. It's common for a coin to fluctuate double-digit percentages within a day, often because of "pump-and-dump" techniques from coordinated users trying to manipulate prices in completely unregulated free markets.

For this reason, none of the investors I spoke with engage in short-term trading but instead choose, in the online parlance of cryptocurrency enthusiasts, to "hodl" (a misppelling of "hold" on a 2013 Bitcoin forum that came to mean "hold on for dear life" rather than sell off for temporary gains). Mr. Dinges and his wife recently bought a house in Los Angeles, but he didn't use his Bitcoins to help with the renovations.

“This is a great opportunity to pull it out and put it toward fixing the house,” he said, “but the future potential is not worth it.”

Mr. Berg would agree, advising BloKtek Capital clients to “set it and forget it” and not fall prey to the temptation to make short-term transactions.

“My wife and I use it as our bank account,” he said. “Every paycheck, we put a percentage into long-term holdings. We do not expect to become rich overnight. That’s a way to become very poor in one hour.” (Though his wife works at his company, it bears mentioning here that the vast majority of cryptocurrency investors seem to be male, and their Twitter discourse tends to be less than refined, with insults often lodged at devotees of rival currencies.)

Even those in it for the long haul, however, admit to monitoring the prices compulsively, scratching the gambler’s itch.

“If I have a moment where the price has left my mind, I’ll want to reinsert it,” Mr. Wax, the record producer, said. “I check it as much as any social media. It’s become as distracting as anything else on my phone.”

As he works in the cryptocurrency world, Mr. Berg maintains an even more observant — and most likely exhausting — regimen.

“I’m always watching the markets,” he said. “The saying is, ‘Crypto never sleeps.’ It’s 24/7, it’s global, it doesn’t have a stock market, it doesn’t have a bell.

“I sleep about four hours a day.”

Beyond its potential long-term financial rewards, many holders of cryptocurrency view it as a vehicle for social change. While many coins have no value beyond serving as a potential alternative currency, or began as larks that have since been popularized by speculators (such as Dogecoin, whose logo is an internet-meme dog and which now has a market capitalization of about $200 million), others — namely Ripple and Ethereum — have meaningful real-world utility and are being adopted by banks and financial institutions.

"The financial gain is fun, but it's really about improving the world, improving the financial system, transparency, cost, increased speed," Mr. Ginn said. "It's the double-sided tape for society. When financial markets collapse, the tape rips people apart and you have a system collapse. Finance got away with it in '08; it almost took the world down, and nothing changed." In lieu of more stringent government oversight, he believes that Ripple can help "reduce systemic risk."

That safety-net altruism drives Yoni Saltzman, 24, who designs robotic mechanisms for aerospace and medical applications. Mr. Saltzman has holdings in four different cryptocurrencies and is working with a small team in New York to develop a digital coin in hopes to introduce within a year. "It's not just about making money," he said. "We like the idea of not only changing the world, but saving the world."

This is, of course, the same vaguely idealistic rationale Silicon Valley executives routinely trot out to justify their ventures, not all of which seem especially concerned with the greater good. In the meantime, those who have boarded the crypto-train frequently proselytize to friends and family. Unsurprisingly, they have more luck with their younger peers. Mr. Guarco, the Duke graduate, has persuaded a few friends to take the plunge.

His older relatives, however, unaccustomed to coins that one can't pluck out of a lint-filled pocket, are a harder sell.

"They usually respond, 'Crypto-what?' " he said.

TEDDY WAYNE'S MOST RECENT NOVEL, "LONER," IS JUST OUT IN PAPERBACK.

Should the Fed Create 'FedCoin' to Rival Bitcoin? A Former Top Official Says 'Maybe'

BY NEIL IRWIN | MAY 4, 2018

If cryptocurrency and blockchain technology really are the future of money, the world's central banks need to get involved, a former Fed governor argues.

MANY ENTHUSIASTS OF Bitcoin and other cryptocurrencies are motivated by deep skepticism of the central banks that control the world's money supply.

But what if central banks themselves entered the game? What would happen if the Federal Reserve, or the European Central Bank or the Bank of Japan used blockchain technology to create their own virtual currencies? Besides, that is, having some cryptocurrency fans' heads explode?

A former Fed governor — who was also a finalist to lead the central bank — thinks the idea deserves serious consideration.

"Most central banks have a view that these crypto-assets are clever, like guys in the garage did it and it's kind of cool, or risky," given the potential investor losses and widespread fraud, said Kevin Warsh, who was a governor at the Fed from 2006 to 2011 and was a top contender to become its chairman late last year when President Trump instead appointed Jerome Powell.

If he had returned to the Fed, Mr. Warsh said, he would have appointed a team "to think about the Fed creating FedCoin, where we would bring legal activities into a digital coin."

"Not that it would supplant and replace cash," he said, "but it would be a pretty effective way when the next crisis happens for us to maybe conduct monetary policy."

He added that blockchain technology, which allows reliable, decentralized record keeping of transactions, could be useful in the payment systems operated by the Fed, which enable the transfer of trillions of dollars between banks.

"It strikes me that a central bank digital currency might have a role to play there," Mr. Warsh, who is now a distinguished visiting fellow at the Hoover Institution at Stanford, told several reporters Thursday evening.

Some central banks are already doing work in this vein, including the Monetary Authority of Singapore and the Bank of England. And Mr. Powell acknowledged the potential applications in his confirmation hearing for the Fed chairmanship in November, saying, "We actually look at blockchain as something that may have significant applications in the wholesale payments part of the economy."

It would be quite a twist if a technology whose most ardent fans are motivated by distrust of central banks became a key tool for those banks.

But it would address some of the concerns connected to Bitcoin and its many privately created rivals. To the degree that the value of existing cryptocurrencies fluctuates wildly, they are ill-suited as a medium of exchange. Central banks have spent hundreds of years learning how to keep the value of money stable.

And to the degree Bitcoin and the like facilitate tax evasion, money laundering and fraud, they will be a target of global law enforcement. Central banks are used to building systems that allow enforcement of those laws.

It's clear that central banks weighing use of blockchain technology don't share the more anarchist impulses of some of the most die-hard cryptocurrency enthusiasts. But there may be more commonality than it might seem. As Mr. Warsh argues, if people really do believe that digital currencies in some form are the future of money, it would behoove central banks to treat them as more than a novelty.

"Congress gave the Fed a monopoly over money," Mr. Warsh said. "And if the next generation of cryptocurrencies look more like money and less like gold — and have less volatility associated with them so they would be not just a speculative asset but could be a reliable unit of account — as a purely defensive matter I wouldn't want somebody to take that monopoly from me."

In other words, if cryptocurrency enthusiasts are correct that this technology could become a better way of carrying out even routine transactions, the Fed and its counterparts are the institutions that have the most to lose.

NEIL IRWIN IS A SENIOR ECONOMICS CORRESPONDENT FOR THE UPSHOT. HE PREVIOUSLY WROTE FOR THE WASHINGTON POST AND IS THE AUTHOR OF "THE ALCHEMISTS: THREE CENTRAL BANKERS AND A WORLD ON FIRE."

Kodak's Dubious Cryptocurrency Gamble

BY KEVIN ROOSE | JAN. 30, 2018

AN EON OR TWO AGO, Eastman Kodak was a bleeding-edge technology company. It hired the smartest engineers and put them to work racking up patents, pioneering new chemical processes and building a globe-spanning camera and film business that, at its peak, employed 145,000 people.

But the digital photo age passed Kodak by, and today, the Rochester, N.Y., company exists mostly in the past tense. Many of the patents have been sold, buildings have been rented out or demolished, and the company has continued to shrink since it filed for bankruptcy in 2012.

Now, the 130-year-old company is trying an unlikely sort of comeback — one built by betting on cryptocurrency. It's a bold gamble that has excited some investors, perplexed others and raised questions about how closely Kodak vetted its cryptocurrency business partners, who now include a paparazzi photo agency, a penny-stock promoter and a company offering that has been called a "magic money making machine."

This month, Kodak lent its name to a digital currency called KodakCoin, which is billed as "a photo-centric cryptocurrency to empower photographers and agencies to take greater control in image rights management." The basic idea behind KodakCoin is to use the blockchain to help photographers manage their collections by creating permanent, immutable records of ownership. The company also struck a licensing deal for a Bitcoin-mining computer called the Kodak KashMiner, which allows users to generate their own cryptocurrency.

Kodak's stock rose more than 200 percent following the announcements, and has not fallen much since.

That's partly because the blockchain — the mathematical ledger system that forms the basis of digital currencies — has a kind of talismanic effect in today's stock market. As investors seek to capitalize

BRETT CARLSEN FOR THE NEW YORK TIMES

Kodak's headquarters in Rochester, N.Y. The 130-year-old company is trying an unlikely sort of comeback built on cryptocurrency.

on the popularity of currencies like Bitcoin and Ethereum, a number of struggling companies have reversed their fortunes, at least temporarily, simply by adding "blockchain" to their names or announcing a new cryptocurrency venture unrelated to their previous line of work. (The most notorious example is Long Island Iced Tea Corp., a beverage company that tripled its value overnight after it rebranded itself "Long Blockchain Corp.")

These sudden, brazen moves have also attracted the attention of regulators. In a recent speech, Jay Clayton, the chairman of the Securities and Exchange Commission, said that the agency was "looking closely at the disclosures of public companies that shift their business models to capitalize on the perceived promise of distributed ledger technology."

Kodak is the most prominent old-line company to enter the cryptocurrency game so far, and maybe the most controversial. Almost

RAMIN RAHIMIAN FOR THE NEW YORK TIMES

Jeff Clarke, Kodak's chief executive, said that the company's blockchain ambitions were genuine.

immediately, critics pounced on the company's plans, characterizing them as a desperate money grab.

"It feels like a publicly traded company issuing a token to raise its stock price from the grave," said Kyle Samani, a partner at the cryptocurrency trading firm Multicoin Capital.

"I would not be sleeping very well if I was involved in this," said Jill Carlson, a blockchain consultant.

In an interview, Jeff Clarke, Kodak's chief executive, said that the company's blockchain ambitions were genuine. He began looking into blockchain technology last summer, he said, and realized that it could solve a perennial problem for photographers — proving ownership of their images, tracking down copyright violators, and getting paid.

"This is not a dog food company that's creating a currency," Mr. Clarke said. "This is a real solution around digital rights management that Kodak has been involved in for many years."

In theory, photographers will be able to upload their images to a platform called KodakOne, create a blockchain-based license for each image, and use web-crawling software to scour the internet looking for copyright violations. Instead of using dollars, photographers can have clients pay them in KodakCoins.

KodakCoin's initial offering, scheduled for Wednesday, is expected to raise as much as $20 million. (On Tuesday night, KodakCoin's website said that it would delay the offering by "several weeks" to verify the credentials of potential investors.) But there are few details about what that money will be used for, or why a similar system could not be built without the blockchain. There is also a more obvious question: Why would photographers want to be paid in digital tokens, rather than cash?

In several calls with KodakCoin leaders, I couldn't get straight answers to these questions. And KodakCoin's white paper, a technical document that details the plans for the currency, is a 40-page mishmash of marketing buzzwords and vague diagrams.

Make no mistake: Digital rights management is a real issue for photographers, and the blockchain does, in theory, offer a compelling solution. But the specific attributes of KodakCoin present some red flags.

First, despite the name, KodakCoin is not actually a Kodak project. The company behind the offering, WENN Digital, is a California-based affiliate of a British photo agency that specializes in paparazzi photo licensing. Under their licensing agreement, Kodak will not receive any direct revenue from the public offering. It will receive a minority stake in WENN Digital, 3 percent of all KodakCoins issued and a royalty on future revenue.

Cameron Chell, a lead adviser to the KodakCoin project, told me that the initial offering represented a "seminal moment" for Kodak, and that the company's interest in blockchain technology was a savvy long-term investment.

"The real story is that it's about to be a renaissance," he said.

But Mr. Chell, a Canadian entrepreneur and motivational speaker who once opened for Tony Robbins, has a troubled track record. In 1998, Mr. Chell agreed to a five-year ban from the Alberta Stock Exchange in Canada and paid a $25,000 fine in connection with a violation of the exchange's rules. A previous company of his ended in ignominy after its chairman was charged with fraud.

Asked about these incidents, Mr. Chell said that he was "young, inexperienced and was irresponsible in my actions," and that he had "learned a lot since 1998 and work hard to conduct myself in a manner that does not reflect that poor judgment." A Kodak spokesman did not return a request for comment about Mr. Chell and whether it knew about the ban.

Mr. Chell has refashioned himself as a blockchain expert in recent years, and KodakCoin is his biggest project so far. He is the chairman of Appcoin Innovations, which was registered as a literary agency — Redstone Literary Agents — until last year, when it became a consulting firm that provides "a turnkey set of services for companies to develop and integrate blockchain and cryptocurrency technologies," according to securities filings.

The company, which trades over the counter as a penny stock, earned no revenue in 2015 or 2016, according to S.E.C. filings. Appcoin Innovations is slated to receive 20 percent of all KodakCoins issued and a portion of the offering proceeds, a stake that could amount to millions if the offering is successful.

"Once formally launched," Mr. Chell wrote to me in an email, "the company will hopefully provide shareholders a traditional and transparent place to participate in the crypto space with projects that are regulatory compliant."

Now, about those coins. You might think that a digital currency that is trying to "democratize photography and make licensing fair to artists," in Mr. Clarke's words, would be easily accessible. But because of regulatory requirements, KodakCoins will be available only to so-called accredited investors in the United States. An accredited investor is defined as a person with a net worth of $1 million or more, or an annual income above $200,000.

How many cryptocurrency-obsessed millionaire photographers do you know?

Even if photographers do meet the requirements to participate, they could have a hard time spending their KodakCoins, or redeeming them for cash. The S.E.C. has warned that securities sold in private offerings, such as KodakCoins, may be difficult to resell — and that investors may be required to hold on to them "indefinitely." A KodakCoin representative told me that the company believes its tokens will eventually be freely traded, and that it may issue other types of tokens in the future that will not be subject to the same restrictions.

KodakCoin's white paper says that token holders may receive other benefits, such as a share of KodakOne's revenue and access to a "marketplace" that will allow them to spend their KodakCoins on camera equipment, studios for photo shoots, and travel expenses. But these benefits could fail to materialize.

Cryptocurrency experts also do not seem impressed with the Kodak KashMiner, a Bitcoin-mining machine advertised at this year's CES electronics trade show. According to the advertisement, users will pay $3,400 to rent the machine, a Kodak-branded computer that solves complex math equations to unlock new Bitcoin, for two years. Half the Bitcoins successfully mined with the Kashminer will go back to Spotlite, the company licensing Kodak's name, and the user will keep the other half.

Kodak hasn't shared many details about its KashMiner deal. But renting the machines could be a hard sell. In its CES advertisement, KashMiner estimates that each renter will earn $9,000 from mining Bitcoin over the two-year contract window. Experts told me that figure was most likely inflated, because Bitcoin mining gets harder over time. And they pointed out that the KashMiner itself appears to simply be a rebranded version of a popular Bitcoin-mining machine that can be purchased outright for less than the rental cost.

All of this — the origins of KodakCoin, the currency itself and the lofty claims about the KashMiner's moneymaking potential — adds up to a big question mark, and points to the possibility that Kodak may be in over its head.

"The best-case scenario is that they believe that the technology will eventually be able to deliver what they've pitched," said Ms. Carlson, the blockchain consultant. "The worst-case scenario is that they are just being very opportunistic."

Mr. Clarke, Kodak's chief executive, characterized the blockchain projects as a small part of the company's overall strategy, and said it was "ironic" that critics were faulting Kodak for embracing a young technology like cryptocurrency, given that its past problems were caused by a failure to innovate.

"This isn't speculative," Mr. Clarke said. "We're taking an emerging new technology in blockchain, and we're using it to solve a real problem."

Solar Experiment Lets Neighbors Trade Energy Among Themselves

BY DIANE CARDWELL | MARCH 13, 2017

BROOKLYN IS KNOWN the world over for things small-batch and local, like designer clogs, craft bourbon and artisanal sauerkraut.

Now, it is trying to add electricity to the list.

In a promising experiment in an affluent swath of the borough, dozens of solar-panel arrays spread across rowhouse rooftops are wired into a growing network. Called the Brooklyn Microgrid, the project is signing up residents and businesses to a virtual trading platform that will allow solar-energy producers to sell excess-electricity credits from their systems to buyers in the group, who may live as close as next door.

The project is still in its early stages — it has just 50 participants thus far — but its implications could be far reaching. The idea is to create a kind of virtual, peer-to-peer energy trading system built on blockchain, the database technology that underlies cryptocurrencies like Bitcoin.

The ability to complete secure transactions and create a business based on energy sharing would allow participants to bypass the electric company energy supply and ultimately build a microgrid with energy generation and storage components that could function on their own, even during broad power failures.

"Community members can work both individually and collectively to help meet demand in an efficient way," said Audrey Zibelman, who recently resigned as chairwoman of the New York State Public Service Commission, which regulates the state's utilities.

"It takes a central procurer — in this case, historically, the utility — out of the mix," she continued, "and really sets the market where they're not buying and selling to the utility but they're identifying each other's need and willingness to buy and sell."

KEVIN HAGEN FOR THE NEW YORK TIMES

Patrick Schnell, a participant in the Brooklyn Microgrid, with solar panels on his roof in Gowanus.

The project is but one example of how rapidly spreading technologies like rooftop solar and blockchain are upending the traditional relationships between electric companies and consumers, putting ever more control in the hands of customers. Across the globe, upstart companies like LO3 Energy, which is designing the Brooklyn experiment with the industrial giant Siemens, are building digital networks that offer the promise of user-driven, decentralized energy systems that can work in tandem with the traditional large-scale grid or, especially in emerging economies, avoid the need for a grid at all.

In Australia, where Ms. Zibelman will soon run the nation's energy markets, a company called Power Ledger announced the start of a residential electricity trading market based in blockchain last year at a housing development in Perth.

In Bangladesh, where an estimated 65 million people lack access to a central grid, ME SOLshare has been developing peer-to-peer trading networks of rural households with and without rooftop solar systems. Producer-consumers there — known as prosumers — can sell excess power into the network, where neighboring homes and businesses can buy it in small increments with a cellphone.

And in Germany, Sonnen, a leading supplier of home batteries and smart energy products and services, has created a web of about 8,000 customers, both with and without solar on their roofs, who are trading their stored energy among one another.

"Peer-to-peer is slowly but surely becoming a reality," said Olaf Lohr, Sonnen's head of United States business development. "This really is a very disruptive technology. The customers are also the owners — they are the producers of the energy. There is no centralized feed-in from one big power plant."

In New York, the Brooklyn microgrid is conceived to work with the conventional grid, which is in the midst of a reboot under Gov. Andrew M. Cuomo's directives to make it more flexible, resilient and economically efficient while reducing greenhouse-gas emissions. That effort, known as Reforming the Energy Vision, or REV, includes encouraging the development of microgrids and more active community participation.

The ideal power system, said Richard L. Kauffman, who as the governor's chairman of energy and finance is leading that effort, is one that combines large power plants and transmission lines with clusters of smaller-scale producer-consumers, "where electrons can flow in more than one direction and supply and demand of electricity is dynamic — and that's different than the grid is today."

The State Public Service Commission has already taken a few of them, including last week approving new ways to determine pricing for electricity from renewable energy projects that more accurately reflect the value to the grid based on geographic location, timing and other factors yet to be determined. But Lawrence Orsini, LO3's chief executive, said the state still needed to determine how to define his company and its network of participants before it could get its market up and running, a move he anticipates by June.

"There's nothing technically infeasible about what we're doing," he said. "In order for transactive energy to take off as a whole, regulators have to be comfortable that markets can actually work this way and, more importantly, that people want markets like this."

Over the past year, LO3 has been working to find those people, using Google Earth to identify homes with rooftop solar installations and then knocking on doors to enlist participants, with some success throughout Park Slope and Gowanus.

On a block of President Street last year, the company carried out two sales of green electricity credits generated by one homeowner's solar system to a neighbor across the street — tiny transactions, but important in proving the concept's viability.

Those sales involved test versions of renewable-energy credits — numbered certificates that are used to track electricity exported from a renewable system to the grid. Utilities, corporations and other customers can buy the credits to claim green energy use.

In the Brooklyn case, LO3 used the credit sales, conducted over PayPal, to test its approach; it cannot legally buy and sell electricity until regulators determine its market status. Once that occurs, Mr. Orsini said, the company will be able to facilitate the trading of energy among its participants — though they would still pay the utility, Con Edison, for infrastructure fees and services, as customers now do when they choose to use a green energy supplier through the utility.

Mr. Orsini's team is busy collecting data from meters installed in prosumer homes, measuring production, use and export of the solar electricity to help model the market. They are also testing a smartphone app that customers will be able to use to manage their electricity purchases, setting parameters to control the source — selecting from a range of conventional, renewable, local and bulk options — as well as how much they are willing to spend.

Mr. Orsini said he expected that most users would want to make their choices and then let the system take over.

KEVIN HAGEN FOR THE NEW YORK TIMES

A Transactive grid meter at Garry Golden's home in Brooklyn.

"No one wants to day-trade energy," he said. "You're giving something to people that they haven't ever had before, and that's really a way to personalize their energy consumption."

That is the aspect that appeals to a number of the participants, including Garry Golden of Windsor Terrace, a futurist who consults for a variety of businesses, including electric utilities and infrastructure companies. Mr. Golden installed solar as part of a group purchase that proved so popular with his neighbors that almost a dozen systems are within view of his roof, forming an attractive cluster for the microgrid experiment.

"We need to make energy a product and a service that people can purchase on their own and not rely on a large centralized entity," Mr. Golden said. He added that it was important to build out infrastructure that would be able to better withstand disasters, both natural and man-made.

Other participants echoed that concern.

"The long-term goal is to be at least partially independent of the grid in emergencies, which was a reasonable argument to join," said Patrick Schnell, whose Gowanus basement flooded during Hurricane Sandy in 2012, though he did not lose power. "Hopefully it will expand and more people will join and it will be more worthwhile."

The project includes plans to create a roughly five-square-block area — either around a collection of public housing projects or near a hospital — that could disconnect from the grid and operate independently in case of a power failure.

"It's a recognition of energy needs beyond your own," Mr. Golden said. "There's a microgrid of our community, and that's great, but the hospitals, the clinics, the schools, large housing complexes — you can feed the energy where it needs to go."

A Former Top Wall Street Regulator Turns to the Blockchain

BY NATHANIEL POPPER | APRIL 22, 2018

SAN FRANCISCO — Gary Gensler was one of the top financial regulators in the Obama administration, the finance chief for Hillary Clinton's 2016 presidential campaign and, before both of those jobs, a partner at Goldman Sachs.

Now, like many other big names from business and government, he is plunging into the world of the blockchain, the data-tracking technology introduced by Bitcoin.

Mr. Gensler, 60, has recently gone to work at the Massachusetts Institute of Technology, where he will write and teach about the potential he sees for blockchains to change the financial world.

He will also use his position to warn about how many of the current projects in the world of virtual currencies, including some of the biggest, are likely to face a significant moment of reckoning with regulators.

Mr. Gensler is set to say in a speech at M.I.T. on Monday that the second and third most widely used virtual currencies, Ether and Ripple, have most likely been issued and traded in violation of American securities regulations.

"There is a strong case for both of them — but particularly Ripple — that they are noncompliant securities," he said in an interview. He believes Bitcoin, the original virtual currency, can remain exempt from securities regulations.

Mr. Gensler will be one of the most influential voices to weigh in on a series of questions that are likely to shape the future of the nascent industry.

The Securities and Exchange Commission and the agency that Mr. Gensler led from 2009 to 2014, the Commodity Futures Trading Commission, are in the middle of determining how to categorize and crack down on many of the virtual currencies created in recent years.

Most of the focus has been on smaller currencies that were issued through so-called initial coin offerings, or I.C.O.s, a method of fund-raising in which entrepreneurs sell custom virtual currencies.

But Mr. Gensler believes that better-known virtual currencies like Ether and Ripple should be in that conversation as well and should likely be categorized as securities, given the way they have been created and sold.

"2018 is going to be a very interesting time," Mr. Gensler said. "Over 1,000 previously issued initial coin offerings, and over 100 exchanges that offer I.C.O.s, are going to need to sort out how to come into compliance with U.S. securities law."

The people behind both Ether and Ripple have argued that their tokens are not securities. But there are signs that the S.E.C. could be receptive to Mr. Gensler's argument. Regulators have indicated in private meetings with industry participants that they are considering whether Ether should be categorized as a security.

All the outstanding Ether were worth around $65 billion at Sunday's price, while the Ripple tokens in the hands of investors are worth around $35 billion.

If they are deemed to be securities, it could become illegal for Americans to trade them on most of the exchanges where they are now traded. That would make it harder to buy and sell them and depress their prices.

Mr. Gensler developed a reputation for standing up to powerful financial interests when he was the head of the Commodity Futures Trading Commission.

Before he got into office, some worried that his background at Goldman Sachs would make him hesitant to take on the big banks. But as the chairman of the commission he became one of the most aggressive watchdogs in the effort to rein in Wall Street after the financial crisis.

Joi Ito, the director of the M.I.T. Media Lab and a member of the board of directors of The New York Times, said the combination of Mr. Gensler's record of independence and his knowledge of finance and policy was what made him so attractive to M.I.T.

Mr. Ito has built the Digital Currency Initiative at the Media Lab in an effort to gather a collection of virtual currency experts who don't have a financial interest in them, though the initiative does provide financial support for some developers working on the Bitcoin software.

"It's important that you have a core group of people who aren't in it for the money, and who care about the proper architecture for the long run," he said.

Mr. Gensler has a dual appointment as a special adviser to the Media Lab and a senior lecturer at the M.I.T. Sloan School of Management, where he will teach a class on the blockchain in the fall.

The original blockchain is the ledger on which all Bitcoin transactions are recorded. The Bitcoin blockchain is updated by a network of computers so that no central authority is needed.

While most blockchain experiments are in an early stage, Mr. Gensler said he had become convinced that blockchains could replace many of the middlemen in the financial industry.

For now, though, his words are likely to have their greatest impact on the quickly evolving debate about how virtual currencies should be regulated.

Most industry experts, including Mr. Gensler, assume that Bitcoin is safe from being categorized as a security because it was not originally issued through an initial coin offering or a central organization, and the software is maintained by a decentralized group of developers. Some other virtual currencies, like Litecoin and Monero, have similar designs.

But Mr. Gensler said Ether could have more problems because the first Ether tokens were sold in 2014, before the network was functional, by the Ethereum Foundation.

Ether could get off the hook, Mr. Gensler said, because its development has been more decentralized recently, and new Ether tokens are now given out to so-called miners through a network.

Aya Miyaguchi, the head of the Ethereum Foundation, said in an email that the foundation "neither controls the supply of nor has the ability to issue Ether, and the quantity of Ether that the foundation holds (under 1 percent of all Ether) is already lower than that held by many other ecosystem participants."

But Mr. Gensler said it would be much harder for the Ripple token, known as XRP, to avoid being categorized as a security. The company that oversees Ripple's development still holds most of the XRP tokens and does most of the work to make the software and the token valuable, he said.

A spokesman for the company Ripple, Tom Channick, said XRP should not be a security.

"XRP does not give its owners an interest or stake in Ripple, and they are not paid dividends," he said. "XRP exists independent of Ripple, was created before the company and will exist after it."

Mr. Gensler, who has no virtual currency investments, said he was not tied to any coin's winning the race. But he does think changes are necessary before blockchains can go mainstream.

"I would be surprised if 10 years from now this isn't somewhere in the financial system in a meaningful way," he said. "But so much of the stuff that is being promoted now will not be around."

A Blockchain Building in Bushwick

BY STUART MILLER | MAY 25, 2018

FROM THE OUTSIDE, 304 Troutman Street in Bushwick, Brooklyn, looks fairly ordinary. In most ways, it is. But this nondescript three-story, five-unit rental building is part of an experiment in using the blockchain technology behind Bitcoin to transform the New York housing market.

"This is going to be a paradigm shift," said Mo Shaikh, a founder of Meridio, a Brooklyn-based company looking to introduce blockchain technology to real estate.

As a secure, decentralized way to register and store payments and transactions online through "smart contracts," blockchain technology will give each of the eight investors who currently own the building cryptocurrency tokens that can be traded and secure access to a crypto-protected database that stores individual transaction data. In theory, the technology will make it nearly impossible for hackers to do widespread damage and will protect against the kind of identity theft that conventional investors might be vulnerable to.

"Blockchain is just an efficient way of asset exchange: The assets can be cryptocurrency, stocks, bonds, art or real estate," said Corbin Page, Mr. Shaikh's partner in Meridio, an offshoot of a larger company called Consensys.

Blockchain is best known as the technology behind Bitcoin, but instead of tracking who owns a digital currency, Meridio's Troutman Street pilot project aims to demonstrate that blockchain can enable online sales of fractional shares of residential or commercial real estate properties.

The experiment at Troutman Street is one of many across the country attempting to move real estate records onto blockchain, and it is part of a larger movement in corporate America to transfer all kinds of records onto blockchain. Many of these experiments promise to

STEFANO UKMAR FOR THE NEW YORK TIMES

Corbin Page, left, and Mo Shaikh founded Meridio, a Brooklyn-based company looking to introduce blockchain technology to the real estate market.

fundamentally change industries, but many have also been plagued by delays and questions about whether and how they will actually be an improvement on the existing systems.

If words like cryptocurrency and blockchain make your eyes glaze over, blockchain boosters point out that a user-friendly system can mean you don't need to fully understand the technology any more than you understand the programming code that allows you to order from Amazon or follow politics on Facebook. You can buy or sell "tokens" — which, in this case, represent shares of a building in cryptocurrency — the same way you would trade online stocks.

Meridio's website will be as easy to use as eTrade and Zillow, Mr. Page said: "We want it to be for everybody. We will have blockchain in the background, giving the efficiency without it being in your face."

In real estate deals, he said, blockchain can reduce paperwork and the need for lawyers and other third parties by allowing people to buy

STEFANO UKMAR FOR THE NEW YORK TIMES

A five-unit rental building in Bushwick, Brooklyn, is the first building where Meridio will turn ownership shares into cryptocurrency tokens.

and sell portions of buildings more efficiently than by crowdfunding or creating LLCs.

Blockchain proselytizers also say that the technology can reduce fraud, speed transactions, lower costs and help democratize real estate.

"Real estate has been slow to adopt new technology, and this is bringing energy and excitement, which is welcome in a staid industry," said Jamie Wiseman, a founder of Cayuga Capital Management, a developer and property manager in Brooklyn and Queens whose holdings include 304 Troutman Street.

Doubters, however, point out that fraud cannot be eliminated so easily and that the primitive title recording system in the United States will thwart modernization efforts. They also raise questions about the effect on neighborhood development and gentrification.

"I am skeptical of some of the claims about the impact of blockchain" on real estate, said Aaron Wright, a professor who created the

Blockchain Project at Benjamin N. Cardozo School of Law and coauthored "Blockchain and the Law: The Rule of Code."

Mr. Wright said that the lack of regulation could lead to volatility in trading and cause rapid changes in neighborhoods. And claims that blockchain can dramatically reduce the hundreds of millions of dollars in annual real estate fraud, he added, may be overblown. While blockchain will make information much less vulnerable to hacks and its instantaneous transaction confirmation could cut down on scams, he said, if fraudulent information enters the system, blockchain is not designed to stop it.

The revolution, if it comes, will likely be gradual.

Mr. Shaikh said they are still teaching Blockchain 101 to most in the real estate industry, through conferences, blog posts and marketing campaigns. And after partnering with the brokerage Cushman & Wakefield, Mr. Page said, it took "20 different conversations to find Cayuga, with executives who understood blockchain's potential and were willing to act."

Cayuga bought 304 Troutman in 2005, and the eight initial investors in the building are now getting cryptocurrency tokens. Starting this summer, they will be able to trade with one another and sell to the tenants there. Meridio is already prepping more properties in New York and beyond, and expects to have them available for trading among accredited investors on their website this summer as well.

"We think blockchain gives us the killer app to make that model work," Mr. Page said. There are no minimums and trading can be done immediately, with lower costs and possibly without a lawyer.

Mr. Shaikh and Mr. Page believe that blockchain will gain traction by allowing people to invest relatively small amounts of money in real estate — unlike crowdfunding and LLCs, which often require a large minimum investment and have "lockup periods" before a property can be flipped. Along with large transfer costs, that has created a high bar for entry to the real estate investment market.

Natalia Karayaneva, the chief executive and founder of Propy, another blockchain company, said this fractionalization of properties could allow investors to buy a piece of high-end homes in Manhattan that are often owned by ultra-wealthy foreign oligarchs.

But Mr. Wright, the Cardozo professor, offered another perspective: The lack of regulation, he said, could mean that foreigners looking to move money out of their home countries and people with "ill-gotten gains" could use the technology to spread their dollars around multiple properties.

Ms. Karayaneva and Meridio's founders, however, believe the fractionalization will bring a bigger and broader pool of capital into real estate. "If you don't have the money to buy your house or apartment, you can buy a piece of it, allowing you to build wealth," Mr. Shaikh said. "That's exciting for middle-class Americans."

There are potential pitfalls, of course — among them, that cryptocurrency has proved quite volatile, and if the value of a home, apartment or retail building were to skyrocket or plummet the way Bitcoin has, the impact could ripple out through an entire neighborhood.

"It depends on how the law plays out with the product, but if there's massive trading without sensible guardrails there'll be potential problems with volatility," Mr. Wright said.

Mr. Page argued that the large scale and tangible nature of real estate should make it less volatile than Bitcoin, and Mr. Shaikh said they would consider implementing rules, like one that allows only a certain number of trades on a property per day, to ease concerns.

But Mr. Wright pointed out that while more capital pouring in from around the world sounded good, if all those people decided New York was the place to invest and that helped drive prices up for local residents, it would "lead to issues on the ground and change the character of a neighborhood."

Mr. Wiseman agreed. "Blockchain may bring costs down," he said, "but it will accelerate gentrification."

There is also the possibility that fractionalization could allow communities to band together to battle gentrification, Mr. Page suggested.

STEFANO UKMAR FOR THE NEW YORK TIMES

Meridio is an offshoot of a larger company called Consensys, based in Bushwick.

Community groups or immigrant-centered organizations, he said, could help coordinate neighbors' efforts to buy up small chunks of apartments or houses, or even commercial real estate.

"Maybe that is a solution," Mr. Wright said, noting that this would have multiple benefits in strengthening a sense of community, although it would take years before it could be widespread.

The effects on individual transactions, however, would be more immediate. Mr. Wright recently ran a demonstration in Australia that showed how smart contracts on blockchain could reduce the "cumbersome half-day process" of a transaction to a matter of minutes.

"It was super exciting," he said, although it would be difficult to implement these changes in the United States, he added, because real estate records here are "very, very fractured" and governed on a county-by-county basis. "Efforts to even digitize records that started in the 1980s haven't fully happened yet."

That is sadly true, said John Mirkovic, deputy recorder of deeds for

Cook County, Ill., which ran a pilot program in Chicago that successfully demonstrated how blockchain technology could be used to more safely and efficiently record real estate transactions.

But many counties around the country still use paper for record-keeping, Mr. Mirkovic said, while more technologically advanced ones may have upgraded to Windows 95.

"Getting people to do something new is not easy," he said. Still, he added, citizens and politicians should push for blockchain as a "good government" issue, making it "a populist technology."

Blockchain Will Be Theirs, Russian Spy Boasted at Conference

BY NATHANIEL POPPER | APRIL 29, 2018

SAN FRANCISCO — Last year, representatives of 25 countries met in Tokyo to work on setting international standards for the blockchain, the technology that was introduced by the virtual currency Bitcoin and has ignited intense interest in corporate and government circles.

Some of the technologists at the meeting of the International Standards Organization were surprised when they learned that the head of the Russian delegation, Grigory Marshalko, worked for the F.S.B., the intelligence agency that is the successor to the K.G.B.

They were even more surprised when they asked the F.S.B. agent why the Russians were devoting such resources to the blockchain standards.

"Look, the internet belongs to the Americans — but blockchain will belong to us," he said, according to one delegate who was there. The Russian added that two other members of his country's four-person delegation to the conference also worked for the F.S.B.

Another delegate who had a separate conversation with the head of the Russian group remembers a slightly different wording: "The internet belonged to America. The blockchain will belong to the Russians."

Both of the delegates who recounted their conversations did so on the condition of anonymity, because discussions at the International Standards Organization, or I.S.O., are supposed to be confidential. Neither the Russian organizations overseeing the delegation to the I.S.O. nor the Russian delegates responded to requests for comment.

The sentiment expressed by the Russian delegate is as clear a sign as any of the significance that some governments are assigning to the blockchain — a technology that is now being applied to things as varied as financial trading and voting — and the degree to which it is becoming a subject of geopolitical battles.

The Russian interest in the normally wonky technical sessions has caused concern among other delegations, who worry that individual countries could push standards that would make the security of the blockchain technology vulnerable to surveillance and attack.

The I.S.O., based in Geneva, was created in 1947 to ensure that important technologies are built or measured in the same way all over the world. Over the years, it has created standards for food safety, film sensitivity and much more.

Russia is not the only country sending high-powered delegations to the I.S.O. technical committee focusing on blockchain standards, which got its start last year. The 25 countries with committee delegations sent over 130 people to the last meeting to discuss matters like a common method for security. China sent officials from the finance ministry while the United States had delegates from IBM and Microsoft, according to participants.

"It is a very sought-out technology today, because it really does create the foundation for the future that is coming," said Gilbert Verdian, the head of the British delegation working on blockchain standards at the I.S.O. and the founder of the company Quant Network. "To get behind it and back it now is going to put people at an advantage, either politically or economically."

The original blockchain is the shared database on which all Bitcoin transactions are recorded. It is kept by a distributed network of computers managed by many people, rather than one central authority. While there are now many virtual currencies, each with its own blockchain, there are also many government and corporate efforts looking at ways to use blockchain technology to securely record other kinds of data.

There are still significant questions about whether the technology will live up to expectations — and few projects have proceeded beyond the pilot stage aside from virtual currency networks like Bitcoin and Ethereum.

But in countries like the United States, China, Russia, Singapore and Switzerland, government groups have talked about using blockchains for myriad tasks, like issuing national currency or tracking identity records for citizens and visitors.

Within the young blockchain industry there is a widespread belief that the companies and countries that establish an early lead could guide the direction of the technology, for both commercial and national security purposes.

Emma Channing, a lawyer who frequently works with blockchain start-ups, recently raised an alarm about the intrigue at the I.S.O. standards group.

Ms. Channing said she was worried that countries that devote more resources to the process could successfully push their preferred cryptographic algorithms to be the standards, potentially creating so-called back doors that could be used in the future to spy on blockchain activity.

"In the context of software it is the perfect Trojan," said Ms. Channing, a co-founder of the Satis Group, an American company that advises blockchain projects. "If something gets buried in it, these things will get adopted wholesale — and won't be questioned on the way in."

Ms. Channing recently emailed dozens of blockchain experts, trying to get them to volunteer as representatives to the I.S.O. delegations in their countries, so that the process does not become dominated by a few countries.

The chairman of the I.S.O. blockchain committee, Craig Dunn, rejected the idea that any country could shape the process. While I.S.O. proceedings are generally confidential, new standards must go through many stages, with many rounds of voting — first with smaller working groups and then with full national delegations.

"There has to be agreement and consensus across the member countries to take a standard forward," said Mr. Dunn, who is also the head of the Australian delegation to the committee.

Few countries have made their interest in the blockchain as clear as Russia. President Vladimir V. Putin met briefly last year with Vitalik Buterin, the founder of Ethereum, the second most widely used blockchain-based virtual currency platform after Bitcoin.

Mr. Putin also put the blockchain at the center of his "Digital Economy" program for Russia, and his government has talked about creating a crypto-ruble, similar to Bitcoin.

One of the Russian delegates to the I.S.O. blockchain group, Maxim Shevchenko, gave a talk last summer in Russia in which he spoke about the country's goals in the I.S.O. group. The bullet points on the slide included "possibility to influence the technology" and "implementation of Russian standards and solutions worldwide."

Another member of the Russian delegation, Alexey Urivskiy, told the Russian newspaper Vedomosti last year that the delegation at the I.S.O. committee was supposed to get Russian cryptographic algorithms into the standard. The Vedomosti article said that the head of the Russian I.S.O. delegation, Mr. Marshalko, was affiliated with the F.S.B.

Russia is not the only country pushing hard on the blockchain. Many Chinese government offices have been public about their interest in taking advantage of the blockchain technology for tasks like tracking people and products moving through industrial supply chains.

At the I.S.O. meetings last fall in Tokyo, the Chinese government sent one of the largest delegations, with at least nine people, including representatives from the finance ministry and the Chinese central bank, according to a delegate from another country who met the Chinese participants.

The United States delegation was led at the last meeting by a Microsoft employee and included a delegate from IBM. Microsoft and IBM are two of the global companies that have pushed hardest to develop blockchain technology.

At the first meeting of the I.S.O. blockchain group, the Russian delegation led a study group on security and privacy issues, which caused discomfort among some delegates from other countries, according to the two delegates who spoke to The New York Times. At a second meeting, oversight for these issues was transferred to a working group led by France.

Mr. Verdian, the head of the British group, said lots of delegations were jockeying to get an edge on the new technology.

"It will change how our society can operate, but at the same time, in harnessing this technology people might want to leverage that for their own gain," he said. "We all owe it to each other to do it right so that it benefits all of us rather than a few."

CHAPTER 4

Editing DNA

In what is considered by many to be the most important discovery in biology, scientists can now edit DNA. Crispr and other gene editing tools enable genome engineers to change the very building blocks of an organism. Excitement over the vast number of possible applications for this technology is tempered by questions about the ethics and effects of using it.

A Powerful New Way to Edit DNA

BY ANDREW POLLACK | MARCH 3, 2014

IN THE LATE 1980s, scientists at Osaka University in Japan noticed unusual repeated DNA sequences next to a gene they were studying in a common bacterium. They mentioned them in the final paragraph of a paper: "The biological significance of these sequences is not known."

Now their significance is known, and it has set off a scientific frenzy.

The sequences, it turns out, are part of a sophisticated immune system that bacteria use to fight viruses. And that system, whose very existence was unknown until about seven years ago, may provide scientists with unprecedented power to rewrite the code of life.

In the past year or so, researchers have discovered that the bacterial system can be harnessed to make precise changes to the DNA of humans, as well as other animals and plants.

This means a genome can be edited, much as a writer might change words or fix spelling errors. It allows "customizing the genome of any cell or any species at will," said Charles Gersbach, an assistant professor of biomedical engineering at Duke University.

Already the molecular system, known as Crispr, is being used to make genetically engineered laboratory animals more easily than could be done before, with changes in multiple genes. Scientists in China recently made monkeys with changes in two genes.

Scientists hope Crispr might also be used for genomic surgery, as it were, to correct errant genes that cause disease. Working in a laboratory — not, as yet, in actual humans — researchers at the Hubrecht Institute in the Netherlands showed they could fix a mutation that causes cystic fibrosis.

But even as it is stirring excitement, Crispr is raising profound questions. Like other technologies that once wowed scientists — like gene therapy, stem cells and RNA interference — it will undoubtedly encounter setbacks before it can be used to help patients.

It is already known, for instance, that Crispr can sometimes change genes other than the intended ones. That could lead to unwanted side effects.

The technique is also raising ethical issues. The ease of creating genetically altered monkeys and rodents could lead to more animal experimentation. And the technique of altering genes in their embryos could conceivably work with human embryos as well, raising the specter of so-called designer babies.

"It does make it easier to genetically engineer the human germ line," said Craig C. Mello, a Nobel laureate at the University of Massachusetts Medical School, referring to making genetic changes that could be passed to future generations.

Still, Crispr is moving toward commercial use. Five academic experts recently raised $43 million to start Editas Medicine, a company in Cambridge, Mass., that aims to treat inherited disease. Other start-ups include Crispr Therapeutics, which is being formed in London, and Caribou Biosciences in Berkeley, Calif.

Agricultural companies might use Crispr to change existing genes in crops to create new traits. That might sidestep the regulations and controversy surrounding genetically engineered crops, which generally have foreign DNA added.

The development of the new tool is an example of the unanticipated benefits of basic research. About 15 years ago, after it became possible to sequence the entire genomes of bacteria, scientists noticed that many species had those repeated DNA sequences that were first noticed a decade earlier in Osaka. They were called "clustered regularly interspaced short palindromic repeats" — Crispr for short. But what was their purpose? In 2007, researchers at Danisco, a company that supplies bacterial cultures used in making cheese and yogurt, confirmed hypotheses that Crispr protects bacteria from viruses.

It is part of an adaptive immune system — one that remembers a pathogen so it is ready the next time that same invader appears. The human adaptive immune system is why people get measles only once and why vaccines work. But it was not imagined that single-cell organisms like bacteria had such systems.

Here is how it works. The repeated DNA sequences in the bacterial genome are separated from one another by other sequences. These "spacers" are excerpts from the sequences of viruses that have attacked the bacterium or its ancestors. They are like genetic mug shots, telling the bacterium which bad guys to watch for. The Crispr defense system will slice up any DNA with that same sequence, so if the same virus invades again, it will be destroyed.

If a previously unseen virus attacks, a new spacer, a new mug shot, is made and put at the end of the chain.

That means the Crispr region "is like a tape recording of exposure to prior invaders," said Erik J. Sontheimer, a Northwestern University professor who helped unravel the mechanism.

And it provides a way to tell two bacterial strains apart, because even two strains from the same species are likely to have encountered different viruses. This is already being used to identify sources of food-poisoning outbreaks.

Cheese and yogurt companies can examine Crispr regions to see if their bacterial cultures are immunized against particular viruses that could slow production.

"Now you can extend the shelf life of that great strain," said Rodolphe Barrangou of North Carolina State University, who previously worked at Danisco and was the lead author on the 2007 paper. "That has changed the game quite a bit for the dairy industry."

The real frenzy, however, started in 2012, when a team led by Emmanuelle Charpentier, then at Umea University in Sweden, and Jennifer A. Doudna of the University of California, Berkeley, demonstrated a way for researchers to use Crispr to slice up any DNA sequence they choose.

Scientists must synthesize a strand of DNA's chemical cousin RNA, part of which matches the DNA sequence to be sliced. This "guide RNA" is attached to a bacterial enzyme called Cas9. When the guide RNA binds to the corresponding DNA sequence, Cas9 cuts the DNA at that site.

The cell tries to repair the cut but often does so imperfectly, which is enough to disable, or knock out a gene. To change a gene, scientists usually insert a patch — a bit of DNA similar to where the break occurred but containing the desired change. That patch is sometimes incorporated into the DNA when the cell repairs the break.

Would this work in organisms besides bacteria? "I knew it was like firing a starting gun in a race," Dr. Doudna said, but sure enough, by early 2013 scientists had shown it would work in human cells, and those of many other animals and plants, even though these species are not known to have Crispr-based immune systems.

"I don't know any species of plant or animal where it has been tried and it failed," said George Church, a professor of genetics at Harvard Medical School. "It allows you to do genome engineering on organisms that are very hard to do otherwise."

In the past, making an animal with multiple genetic changes usually required creating separate animals with single changes and then crossbreeding them to produce offspring with multiple changes. With Crispr, multiple genetic changes can be made in one step, by putting multiple guide RNAs into the cell.

"It just completely changes the landscape," Dr. Doudna said. Berkeley scientists used to farm out that work to specialized laboratories or companies. Now, she said, "people are able to make mice in their own labs."

There are other techniques that can do what Crispr does, though Crispr is "the easiest by far," Dr. Church said.

RNA interference, for instance, can silence particular genes. It is similar to Crispr in that it also uses RNA that matches the gene to be silenced.

But RNA interference works by inhibiting messenger RNA, which translates a gene into a protein. That usually provides only a partial and temporary disabling of the gene, because the cell can make new messenger RNA. Crispr disables the gene itself, potentially a more complete and permanent inactivation.

There are also already ways to change genes, namely zinc-finger nucleases and transcription activator-like effector nucleases, or Talens. The biotechnology company Sangamo BioSciences is already conducting a clinical trial of a treatment for H.I.V. that uses zinc fingers to alter patients' immune cells to make them resistant to the virus.

Both techniques use proteins to guide where the DNA is cut; it is more difficult to develop a protein that binds to a specific DNA sequence than it is to make a piece of RNA with the matching sequence.

With zinc fingers "it might take you months or years to get something to work well for one gene," said Dr. Gersbach at Duke. With Crispr, "it takes days to weeks."

Quick is not always accurate, however. While Crispr is generally precise, it can have off-target effects, cutting DNA at places where the sequence is similar but not identical to that of the guide RNA.

Crispr "may not yet have adequate specificity to completely displace" the older techniques, Dana Carroll, a biochemistry professor at the University of Utah, wrote in a commentary in Nature Biotechnology in September.

Still, scientists are already figuring out how to make Crispr more specific.

Another obstacle for treating diseases will be the delivery of the genetic changes to all the cells in the body that need it.

For some diseases, it may be possible to extract blood stem cells from the body, alter them using Crispr, and put them back. If that is not possible, the DNA needed to make Cas9, the guide RNA and the corrective patch might be put into a disabled virus. This technique is used for gene therapy, but does not always work well.

It is likely to be a few years before Crispr is tested in people. For now, there is a lot more to learn about it.

Chase L. Beisel at North Carolina State reported that Crispr could be used to kill one strain of bacteria in a mixture of strains, by targeting a sequence unique to that strain. That might one day lead to antibiotics that can kill the bad bugs without also killing the good ones.

David S. Weiss of Emory University found that some bacteria use Cas9 to silence one of their own genes, rather than that of a virus, to help them evade detection by their host's immune system.

The pace of new discoveries and applications is dizzying. "All of this has basically happened in a year," Dr. Weiss said. "It's incredible."

Jennifer Doudna, a Pioneer Who Helped Simplify Genome Editing

BY ANDREW POLLACK | MAY 11, 2015

BERKELEY, CALIF. — As a child in Hilo, one of the less touristy parts of Hawaii, Jennifer A. Doudna felt out of place. She had blond hair and blue eyes, and she was taller than the other kids, who were mostly of Polynesian and Asian descent.

"I think to them I looked like a freak," she recently recalled. "And I felt like a freak."

Her isolation contributed to a kind of bookishness that propelled her toward science. Her upbringing "toughened her up," said her husband, Jamie Cate. "She can handle a lot of pressure."

These days, that talent is being put to the test.

Three years ago, Dr. Doudna, a biochemist at the University of California, Berkeley, helped make one of the most monumental discoveries in biology: a relatively easy way to alter any organism's DNA, just as a computer user can edit a word in a document.

The discovery has turned Dr. Doudna (the first syllable rhymes with loud) into a celebrity of sorts, the recipient of numerous accolades and prizes. The so-called Crispr-Cas9 genome editing technique is already widely used in laboratory studies, and scientists hope it may one day help rewrite flawed genes in people, opening tremendous new possibilities for treating, even curing, diseases.

But now Dr. Doudna, 51, is battling on two fronts to control what she helped create.

While everyone welcomes Crispr-Cas9 as a strategy to treat disease, many scientists are worried that it could also be used to alter genes in human embryos, sperm or eggs in ways that can be passed from generation to generation. The prospect raises fears of a dystopian future in which scientists create an elite population of designer babies with enhanced intelligence, beauty or other traits.

MATT EDGE FOR THE NEW YORK TIMES

Dr. Jennifer A. Doudna, who helped make one of the most monumental discoveries in biology.

Scientists in China reported last month that they had already used the technique in an attempt to change genes in human embryos, though on defective embryos and without real success.

Dr. Doudna has been organizing the scientific community to prevent this ethical line from being crossed. "The idea that you would affect evolution is a very profound thing," she said.

She is also fighting for control of what could be hugely lucrative intellectual property rights to the genome editing technique. To the surprise of many, the first sweeping patents for the technology were granted not to her, but to Feng Zhang, a scientist at the Broad Institute and M.I.T.

The University of California is challenging the decision, and the nasty skirmish has cast a bit of a pall over the field.

"I really want to see this technology used to help people," Dr. Doudna said. "It would be a shame if the I.P. situation would block that."

The development of the Crispr-Cas9 technique is a story in which obscure basic biological research turned out to have huge practical implications. For Dr. Doudna, though, it is only one accomplishment in a stellar career.

"She's been a high-impact scientist from the time she was a graduate student," said Thomas Cech, a Nobel laureate and professor of chemistry and biochemistry at the University of Colorado, for whom Dr. Doudna was a postdoctoral researcher. "New topics, new fields of science, but she just has a knack for discovery."

A 'DUMBSTRUCK' MOMENT

Dr. Doudna was 7 when she moved to Hilo, where her father taught literature at the University of Hawaii campus there, and her mother lectured on history at a community college. Their daughter loved exploring the rain forests and was fascinated by how things worked. She found her calling in high school after hearing a lecture by a scientist about her research into how normal cells became cancerous.

"I was just dumbstruck," Dr. Doudna recalled. "I wanted to be her."

After studying biochemistry at Pomona College in California, she went to Harvard for graduate school. There her adviser, the future Nobel laureate Jack Szostak, was doing research on RNA. Some scientists believe that RNA, not DNA, was the basis of early life, since the molecule can both store genetic information and catalyze chemical reactions.

Dr. Doudna earned her doctoral degree by engineering a catalytic RNA that could self-replicate, adding evidence to that theory. But her inability to visualize this catalytic RNA hindered her work.

So as a postdoctoral researcher in Colorado, she decided to try to determine the three-dimensional atomic structure of RNA using X-ray diffraction — and succeeded, though she had had no formal training in the technique. Structural and biochemical studies of RNA in action have been her forte ever since.

In 2000, while on the faculty at Yale, she won the Alan T. Waterman Award, given each year by the National Science Foundation to an exceptional young scientist. She moved to Berkeley in 2002.

In 2005, Dr. Doudna was approached by Jillian Banfield, an environmental researcher at Berkeley who had been sequencing the DNA of unusual microbes that lived in a highly acidic abandoned mine. In the genomes of many of these microbes were unusual repeating sequences called "clustered regularly interspaced short palindromic repeats," or Crispr.

No one was quite sure what they did, though over the next few years scientists elsewhere established that these sequences were part of a bacterial immune system. Between the repeated sequences were stretches of DNA taken from viruses that had previously infected the bacteria — genetic most-wanted posters, so to speak.

If the same virus invaded again, these stretches of DNA would permit the bacteria to recognize it and destroy it by slicing up its genetic material. Dr. Doudna was trying to figure out exactly how this happened.

"I remember thinking this is probably the most obscure thing I ever worked on," she said.

It would prove to have wide use. At a conference in early 2011, she met Emmanuelle Charpentier, a French microbiologist at Umea University in Sweden, who had already made some fundamental discoveries about the relatively simple Crispr system in one bacterial species.

The bacterial expert and the structural biologist decided to work together.

"It was very enjoyable, because we were complementary," said Dr. Charpentier, who recalled sitting in her office near the North Pole while Dr. Doudna regaled her with stories about Hawaii.

Along with postdoctoral researchers Martin Jinek and Krzysztof Chylinski, the two scientists eventually figured out how two pieces of RNA join up with a protein made by the bacteria called Cas9 to cut DNA at a specific spot. The researchers also found that the two RNA pieces could be combined into one and still function.

In a eureka moment, the scientists realized that this cellular defense system might be used to edit genomes, not just kill viruses.

A specific sequence of guide RNA could be made to attach to a spot virtually anywhere on the genome, and the Cas9 protein would cleave the DNA at that spot. Then pieces of the DNA could be deleted or added, just as a film editor might cut a film and splice in new frames.

The researchers demonstrated this using DNA in a test tube. While there were other genome editing techniques, they found that Crispr-Cas9 was much simpler.

The paper describing the technique, published by the journal Science in June 2012, set off a race to see if it would work in human, plant and animal cells.

Dr. Doudna, whose expertise was in working with molecules, not cells, reported such a demonstration in human cells in January 2013. But her report came four weeks after two papers were published simultaneously, one by George Church at Harvard and the other by the Broad Institute's Dr. Zhang.

THE PATENT FIGHT

Now the University of California and the Broad Institute are arguing before the federal patent office over whether Dr. Doudna or Dr. Zhang, who last year received the Waterman Award for young scientists that Dr. Doudna had won years earlier, was the first to invent the genome editing technique. So far, the patents have gone to Dr. Zhang.

The Broad Institute claims that the paper by Dr. Doudna and Dr. Charpentier in 2012 did not demonstrate how to alter DNA in cells with nuclei, including human cells, something requiring the inventive steps that Dr. Zhang took. His patent application included pages from a lab notebook he said demonstrated that he was doing Crispr genome editing even before the 2012 paper was published.

The University of California says it filed for a patent months before Dr. Zhang did, though the Broad Institute says that initial application lacked necessary details. The university's request to the patent office says that once the 2012 paper laid out the recipe, it was obvious how to use it in cells. The university also says Dr. Zhang's notebook does not prove he could edit genomes before the 2012 paper.

Patent disputes are often settled in time. In any event, Dr. Church of Harvard said, before Crispr-Cas9 could be used to treat disease, it would need important refinements from many other researchers.

"It's going to be hard to use Feng's without Jennifer's, and it would be hard to use either of them without further improvements," he said.

The scientists have formed competing companies with rights to their patents and pending patents. Dr. Doudna co-founded Caribou Biosciences to work on research uses of Crispr-Cas9, and more recently, Intellia Therapeutics to work on disease treatments.

Dr. Church and Dr. Zhang are co-founders of Editas Medicine, which Dr. Doudna also helped start but then withdrew from. Dr. Charpentier, who is now at the Helmholtz Center for Infection Research in Germany, helped start Crispr Therapeutics. She and Dr. Doudna remain friends, but no longer collaborate on research.

Even before the dust settles, researchers are moving ahead. While contending with the patents, Dr. Doudna began hearing reports that researchers were trying to use Crispr-Cas9 to make inheritable DNA changes in embryos. Genetically altered monkeys had already been created in China using the technique.

"It's very far afield from the kind of chemistry I think about and know about," she said. Still, she felt it would be irresponsible to ignore the rumors.

She organized a meeting of leading biologists in Napa, Calif., in January. In a subsequent commentary published in Science, the group called for a moratorium on attempts to create altered babies, though they said basic research on inheritable changes should still be done.

Dr. Doudna said it was not practical to prohibit basic research. "You can't really put a lid on it, even if you wanted to," she said. She and others are trying to organize a bigger international meeting with participants from companies and governments as well as universities, possibly to set new guidelines.

LEARNING TO LIVE WITH FAME

She is also trying to cope with her newfound quasi-celebrity status. She has been invited to hobnob with entrepreneurs in Silicon Valley, to speak to science fiction writers, to advise Hollywood on science-themed movies. The garden, her hobby, has had to wait.

In November, Dr. Doudna and Dr. Charpentier were each awarded $3 million Breakthrough Prizes, endowed by leading internet entrepreneurs. They accepted their awards at an Oscars-like black-tie affair attended by movie stars like Cameron Diaz and Benedict Cumberbatch. Recently Time magazine listed the two scientists among the 100 most influential people in the world.

Dr. Doudna, who has a 12-year-old son, Andrew, also finds herself a role model for women in science. Her secret: "I have a great partner," with whom she shares the chores.

Her husband, Dr. Cate, is also a professor at Cal-Berkeley. The couple have adjacent offices, with views of the Golden Gate Bridge in the distance. Dr. Cate also studies RNA; there is some overlap, but mostly they do their own research. Andrew walks to their office from his middle school each afternoon and hangs out until his parents are ready to go home.

"I don't think of myself as a role model, but I can see that I am," Dr. Doudna said. "I still think of myself as that person back in Hawaii."

Gene Drives Offer New Hope Against Diseases and Crop Pests

BY NICHOLAS WADE | DEC. 21, 2015

BIOLOGISTS IN THE United States and Europe are developing a revolutionary genetic technique that promises to provide an unprecedented degree of control over insect-borne diseases and crop pests.

The technique involves a mechanism called a gene drive system, which propels a gene of choice throughout a population. No gene drives have yet been tested in the wild, but in laboratory organisms like the fruit fly, they have converted almost the entire population to carry the favored version of a gene.

Gene drives "could potentially prevent the spread of disease, support agriculture by reversing pesticide and herbicide resistance in insects and weeds, and control damaging invasive species," a group of Harvard biologists wrote last year in the journal eLIFE.

A much discussed application of gene drives would help rid the world of pest-borne diseases like malaria, dengue fever and Lyme disease.

A gene drive designed to render a population extinct is known as a crash drive. A crash drive being developed for mosquitoes consists of a gene engineered into the Y chromosome that shreds the X chromosome in the cells that make the mosquito's sperm, thus ensuring that all progeny are male. Unless the drive itself is damaged through mutation, the number of females would be expected to dwindle each generation until the population collapses.

Biologists led by Andrea Crisanti and Tony Nolan at Imperial College London reported this month in the journal Nature Biotechnology their development of mosquitoes with gene drives that disrupt three genes for female fertility, each of which acts at a different stage of egg formation. Because the female mosquitoes are infertile only when a copy is inherited from both parents, the gene drives would be thoroughly disseminated through a population before taking their toll.

URIEL SINAI FOR THE NEW YORK TIMES

A woman in Tanzania under a mosquito tent with a relative who was being treated for malaria. With gene drives, it may be possible to kill off a mosquito population or make the population resistant to malaria parasites.

They could "suppress mosquito populations to levels that do not support malaria transmission," the authors wrote.

The mosquitoes are not yet ready for release. Because natural selection will heavily favor any wild mosquitoes that acquire resistance to the gene drives, the researchers need to prevent such resistance from arising. One approach would be to target two or three sites in the same fertility gene, giving natural selection a much higher barrier to overcome.

Another approach is to endow mosquitoes with genes that make them resistant to the malaria parasite. Last month, biologists at the Irvine and San Diego campuses of the University of California reported introducing a gene drive with a cargo of malaria-resistance genes into mosquitoes. Such genes, if successfully propelled throughout a wild mosquito population, would render a region free of the malarial parasite, which could no longer spread via mosquito bites.

In agriculture, biologists envisage gene drive systems that could destroy or modify insect pests, and reverse genetic resistance to pesticides in species that had acquired it. Gene drives may also be used to squelch populations of harmful invasive species like rats.

Gene drives have two major technical limitations. They will work only in sexually reproducing species, which effectively rules out bacteria. Second, they spread significantly only in species that reproduce quickly, meaning they would be of no practical use in elephants or people.

Because no gene drive organisms have yet been released, biologists cannot yet assess how well they will work and what degree of risk they may pose.

The issue of risk, rather than effectiveness, has dominated discussion for the last several months. Biologists are eager to see the benefits of the technology realized, and wish to avoid any consequences that might erode public confidence or get gene drive systems off on the wrong foot, as has happened with genetically modified foods. Several articles published in the last few months propose specific safety precautions and call for full public discussion of gene drives, along with speedy regulation.

Because a single escaped organism carrying a gene drive system "could alter a substantial fraction of the wild population with unpredictable ecological consequences, the decision to deploy a gene drive must be made collectively by society," a group of scientists, led by George M. Church of Harvard Medical School, said in Nature Biotechnology last month.

A GENE EDITING ADVANCE

A gene drive refers to any process that biases the usual pattern of Mendelian inheritance, in which a gene has a 50 percent chance of making it to the next generation. Several gene drive processes exist in nature but are hard to manipulate.

In 2003, Austin Burt, a biologist at a branch of Imperial College London in Sunninghill, England, essentially laid out the whole theory of gene drives and their possible applications based on natural gene drives known as homing endonucleases. "Clearly, the technology described here is not to be used lightly," he concluded. "Given the suffering caused by some species, neither is it obviously one to be ignored."

An endonuclease is an enzyme that cuts at a specific site the DNA of the chromosome with which its gene's own chromosome is paired. Because DNA breaks are very threatening to genome integrity, cells rush to repair them, often by using the other chromosome of a pair as a template. In doing so, they copy the gene for the endonuclease into the joint made between the two broken ends of the cut chromosome. If this repair occurs in a germ line cell, both eggs and sperm will carry the endonuclease gene together with any cargo genes that genetic engineers may have attached to it.

Because it is hard to change the natural site at which a homing endonuclease cuts DNA, Dr. Burt's proposed gene drive systems could not easily be put into practice. All that changed three years ago with the invention of Crispr-Cas9 gene editing. The technique is based on a natural system that evolved in bacteria as a defense against invading viruses.

The bacteria store DNA samples from these invasive viruses in a DNA library, called Crispr, that is part of their genome. When a virus attacks, endonucleases such Cas9 (Cas stands for Crispr-associated) are primed by the Crispr library to cut viral DNA of the same sequence.

After recovering from their amazement that organisms as small as bacteria possessed an adaptive immune system, biologists realized that they could take over the Cas9 endonuclease and make it cut DNA at any site of their choosing by providing it with a synthetic guide sequence instead of one from the Crispr library. The use of Crispr-Cas9 for genome editing was first published in 2012 by Jennifer Doudna of the University of California, Berkeley, and Emmanuelle Charpentier, now at the Max Planck Institute for Infection Biology in Berlin. But Feng Zhang, of the Broad Institute in Cambridge, Mass., was the first to file a patent, which Berkeley lawyers are challenging.

The Crispr-Cas9 technique gives biologists unprecedented power to edit DNA. With the ability to cut DNA at a specific site, they can let the cell's DNA repair machinery paste in new sequences, usually a gene of interest, in the process of annealing the two cut ends of the DNA molecule.

UNCERTAIN ECOLOGICAL EFFECT

In April, two biologists at the University of California, San Diego, Valentino M. Gantz and Ethan Bier, caused a stir with a gene drive system that carried a gene for albinism into laboratory fruit flies. Their drive was astonishingly efficient: Within two generations, some 97 percent of the fruit flies had been rendered pale by the mutation. Although gene drives may not spread so quickly in natural populations, which are more variable, the experiment demonstrated the vast potential of the method for modifying pest populations.

With the Crispr-Cas9 technique, laboratories all over the world, including many with no experience in confining potentially hazardous organisms, could now generate gene drive systems. A flurry of articles urging caution began to appear from other biologists, who noted that if a fruit fly with a gene drive system escaped from a laboratory, it could affect fruit flies worldwide. In an article in Science in August, Dr. Church and others recommended steps for avoiding accidental release, including having more than one confinement strategy. With strong safeguards, they wrote, "we hope to build a foundation of public trust for potential future applications."

A harder issue than containment is how to assess the ecological effect of gene drive systems. Even something as apparently benign as eliminating mosquitoes could have ecological effects "because mosquitoes interact with other species," said Kevin Esvelt, a biochemist at Harvard. Dr. Burt, however, noted in an interview that there are more than 800 species of mosquitoes in Africa, and eliminating the group of species that carries malaria was "unlikely to have a cascading effect," even though the possibility should be looked at. Dr. Burt said he is also unable to think of any disadvantage to humans or to mosquitoes in eliminating the malaria parasite that preys on both.

Another concern is that a gene drive system may have unintended consequences, by making its target species more pathogenic or by spreading to other species. A suggested approach to this problem is to proceed in careful stages, releasing a gene drive system first in a caged population of target insects, and then in an isolated habitat like an island, if possible, before any major release into the wild.

A PLAN FOR BACKING OUT

It may seem that once a gene drive system is released, it can never be recalled. But this may not be entirely true. Biologists are working on the concepts of "reversal drives" and "immunizing drives." A reversal drive would cut out an errant drive and restore the target organism almost to its previous state. An immunizing drive would attack and pre-emptively change the DNA sequence targeted by the rogue drive.

A group of biologists proposed last year that before any gene drive system is released into the environment, its designers should prepare a standby reversal drive. But critics suggested that the availability of reversal drives might make people overconfident — and in any case, they might not work as advertised.

"If your first drive doesn't work as intended, are you sure your second drive will work?" Dr. Burt said.

The power over nature that gene drive systems promise is a responsibility that surely no biologist takes lightly. But people already exert control over nature with a slew of toxic pesticides and herbicides that are a heavy burden on the environment. Gene drive systems offer a much more specific and less harmful approach, at least in principle, toward attaining the same goals.

Risks aside, there is no guarantee that gene drives will work as well in the field as they do in the laboratory. Wild populations of mosquitoes, say, may have much genetic variation at the target site of a gene drive system. Those with a variant target site would escape the drive and might have a selective advantage over it.

Resistance will arise, as to any change that reduces a species's fitness. But biologists could respond by releasing many drives into a wild population, each assigned to a different target. Even if a drive comes to dominate a whole population, biologists expect it will eventually be eliminated by fitter genes. But a response would be to keep releasing new drives.

"I think we'll be able to make this work," Dr. Burt said.

Scientists Find Form of Crispr Gene Editing With New Capabilities

BY CARL ZIMMER | JUNE 3, 2016

JUST A FEW YEARS AGO, Crispr was a cipher — something that sounded to most ears like a device for keeping lettuce fresh. Today, Crispr-Cas9 is widely known as a powerful way to edit genes. Scientists are deploying it in promising experiments, and a number of companies are already using it to develop drugs to treat conditions ranging from cancer to sickle-cell anemia.

Yet there is still a lot of misunderstanding around it. Crispr describes a series of DNA sequences discovered in microbes, part of a system to defend against attacking viruses. Microbes make thousands of forms of Crispr, most of which are just starting to be investigated by scientists. If they can be harnessed, some may bring changes to medicine that we can barely imagine.

On Thursday, in the journal Science, researchers demonstrated just how much is left to discover. They found that an ordinary mouth bacterium makes a form of Crispr that breaks apart not DNA, but RNA — the molecular messenger used by cells to turn genes into proteins.

If scientists can get this process to work in human cells, they may open up a new front in gene engineering, gaining the ability to precisely adjust the proteins in cells, for instance, or to target cancer cells.

"The groundbreaking thing about this work is that it now opens up the RNA world to Crispr," said Oliver Rackham, a synthetic biologist at the University of Western Australia who was not involved in the study.

Crispr was first discovered in 1987, but it took decades for scientists to figure out that microbes needed the system to recognize DNA from invading viruses and to chop it into pieces, stopping the infection.

In 2012, a team of scientists led by Jennifer Doudna of the University of California, Berkeley, and Emmanuelle Charpentier, then at Umea

University in Sweden, discovered how to use this microbial defense as a gene-editing tool that could potentially alter any piece of DNA.

Most of that early work was carried out with Crispr molecules from a species of bacteria that lives in human skin called Streptococcus pyogenes. Once those molecules proved effective at reassembling human DNA, a number of scientists began looking at other species for Crispr systems that might be even better.

Some researchers investigated familiar species that have been studied in labs for decades. But Eugene V. Koonin and his colleagues at the National Center for Biotechnology Information instead scoured databases containing hundreds of millions of genetic sequences for those that resembled Crispr genes.

Once they discovered some candidates, they joined forces with Feng Zhang of M.I.T., who published one of the first studies on using Crispr to edit human DNA. One of the first candidates they looked at came from a species of bacteria that lives in the mouth, known as Leptotrichia shahii.

It had a group of genes that looked like Crispr genes in some ways, but with stark differences. When the researchers equipped bacteria with these genes, which they called C2c2, they found that the organisms gained a defense that had never been seen.

Many viruses do not contain DNA. Instead, their genetic information is encoded in RNA, DNA's single-stranded cousin, which they use to hijack the genes of their hosts and cause them to make new viruses. Some of these RNA viruses, such as H.I.V. and poliovirus, attack our species. Many others attack bacteria.

Previously discovered Crispr molecules are very good at whacking apart DNA but don't protect bacteria from an RNA virus. Dr. Zhang and his colleagues discovered that bacteria with C2c2 make molecules that can attack RNA and chop it up, destroying the invaders.

The researchers also found that they could tailor these genes to cut any RNA molecule they wanted. Now they are tinkering with the process to try to get it to work in human cells.

"There could be a lot of cool applications," Dr. Zhang said. He hopes, for example, that C2c2 molecules could be trained to destroy RNA made only in cancer cells. Those cells would be unable to make essential proteins and die.

While it remains to be seen if these will become useful tools, Dr. Koonin said, the discovery has already revealed something important about the evolutionary history of these microbial defenses.

Some parts of C2c2 genes share a common evolutionary origin with the defense systems seen in other bacterial species. Over billions of years, Dr. Koonin said, evolution has blindly tinkered with these genes in order to generate new ways to protect against viruses.

Exploring this evolution is more productive for now than trying to design gene-editing technology from scratch, Dr. Zhang said. "We're not quite smart enough yet," he added.

In fact, some future advances in gene editing may even not be based on Crispr. Microbes have evolved several different lines of defense against viruses, some of which are only now coming to light.

In recent years, for example, scientists have discovered that microbes can use another group of proteins, called Argonautes, to chop up viral DNA. Last month, a team of Chinese researchers announced that they were able to use Argonaute proteins to edit DNA in human cells.

Paul S. Knoepfler, a cell biologist at the University of California, Davis, is taking a wait-and-see attitude about Argonaute proteins, but he said he would not be surprised if they quickly turned out to be yet another powerful gene-editing tool.

"This field seems to move in dog years," he said. "It feels like seven times faster than real time."

In Breakthrough, Scientists Edit a Dangerous Mutation From Genes in Human Embryos

BY PAM BELLUCK | AUG. 2, 2017

SCIENTISTS FOR THE first time have successfully edited genes in human embryos to repair a common and serious disease-causing mutation, producing apparently healthy embryos, according to a study published on Wednesday.

The research marks a major milestone and, while a long way from clinical use, it raises the prospect that gene editing may one day protect babies from a variety of hereditary conditions.

But the achievement is also an example of human genetic engineering, once feared and unthinkable, and is sure to renew ethical concerns that some might try to design babies with certain traits, like greater intelligence or athleticism.

Scientists have long feared the unforeseen medical consequences of making inherited changes to human DNA. The cultural implications may be just as disturbing: Some experts have warned that unregulated genetic engineering may lead to a new form of eugenics, in which people with means pay to have children with enhanced traits even as those with disabilities are devalued.

The study, published in the journal Nature, comes just months after a national scientific committee recommended new guidelines for modifying embryos, easing blanket proscriptions but urging the technique be used only for dire medical problems.

"We've always said in the past gene editing shouldn't be done, mostly because it couldn't be done safely," said Richard Hynes, a cancer researcher at the Massachusetts Institute of Technology who co-led the committee. "That's still true, but now it looks like it's going to be done safely soon," he said, adding that the research is "a big breakthrough."

"What our report said was, once the technical hurdles are cleared, then there will be societal issues that have to be considered and discussions that are going to have to happen. Now's the time."

Scientists at Oregon Health and Science University, with colleagues in California, China and South Korea, reported that they repaired dozens of embryos, fixing a mutation that causes a common heart condition that can lead to sudden death later in life.

If embryos with the repaired mutation were allowed to develop into babies, they would not only be disease-free but also would not transmit the disease to descendants.

The researchers averted two important safety problems: They produced embryos in which all cells — not just some — were mutation-free, and they avoided creating unwanted extra mutations.

"It feels a bit like a 'one small step for (hu)mans, one giant leap for (hu) mankind' moment," Jennifer Doudna, a biochemist who helped discover the gene-editing method used, called CRISPR-Cas9, said in an email.

"I expect these results will be encouraging to those who hope to use human embryo editing for either research or eventual clinical purposes," said Dr. Doudna, who was not involved in the study.

Much more research is needed before the method could be tested in clinical trials, currently impermissible under federal law. But if the technique is found to work safely with this and other mutations, it might help some couples who could not otherwise have healthy children.

Potentially, it could apply to any of more than 10,000 conditions caused by specific inherited mutations. Researchers and experts said those might include breast and ovarian cancer linked to BRCA mutations, as well as diseases like Huntington's, Tay-Sachs, beta thalassemia, and even sickle cell anemia, cystic fibrosis or some cases of early-onset Alzheimer's.

"You could certainly help families who have been blighted by a horrible genetic disease," said Robin Lovell-Badge, a professor of genetics and embryology at the Francis Crick Institute in London, who was not involved in the study.

Gene Editing in Embryos

Scientists tried two techniques to remove a dangerous mutation. In the first, genetic "scissors" were inserted into fertilized eggs. The mutation was repaired in some of the resulting embryos but not always in every cell. The second method worked better: By injecting the "scissors" along with the sperm into the egg, more embryos emerged with repaired genes in every cell.

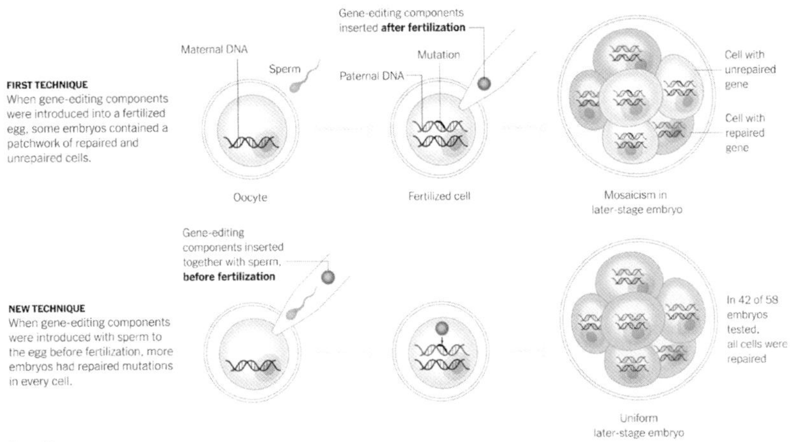

Source: Nature

THE NEW YORK TIMES

"You could quite imagine that in the future the demand would increase. Maybe it will still be small, but for those individuals it will be very important."

The researchers also discovered something unexpected: a previously unknown way that embryos repair themselves.

In other cells in the body, the editing process is carried out by genes that copy a DNA template introduced by scientists. In these embryos, the sperm cell's mutant gene ignored that template and instead copied the healthy DNA sequence from the egg cell.

"We were so surprised that we just couldn't get this template that we made to be used," said Shoukhrat Mitalipov, director of the Center for Embryonic Cell and Gene Therapy at Oregon Health and Science University and senior author of the study. "It was very new and unusual."

The research significantly improves upon previous efforts. In three sets of experiments in China since 2015, researchers seldom managed to get the intended change into embryonic genes.

And some embryos had cells that did not get repaired — a phenomenon called mosaicism that could result in the mutation being passed on — as well as unplanned mutations that could cause other health problems.

In February, a National Academy of Sciences, Engineering and Medicine committee endorsed modifying embryos, but only to correct mutations that cause “a serious disease or condition” and when no “reasonable alternatives” exist.

Sheldon Krimsky, a bioethicist at Tufts University, said the main uncertainty about the new technique was whether “reasonable alternatives” to gene editing already exist.

As the authors themselves noted, many couples use pre-implantation genetic diagnosis to screen embryos at fertility clinics, allowing only healthy ones to be implanted. For these parents, gene editing could help by repairing mutant embryos so that more disease-free embryos would be available for implantation.

Hank Greely, director of the Center for Law and the Biosciences at Stanford, said creating fewer defective embryos also would reduce the number discarded by fertility clinics, which some people oppose.

The larger issue is so-called germline engineering, which refers to changes made to embryo that are inheritable.

“If you’re in one camp, it’s a horror to be avoided, and if you’re in the other camp, it’s desirable,” Dr. Greely said. “That’s going to continue to be the fight, whether it’s a feature or a bug.”

For now, the fight is theoretical. Congress has barred the Food and Drug Administration from considering clinical trials involving germline engineering. And the National Institutes of Health is prohibited from funding gene-editing research in human embryos. (The new study was funded by Oregon Health and Science University, the Institute for Basic Science in South Korea, and several foundations.)

The authors say they hope that once the method is optimized and studied with other mutations, officials in the United States or another country will allow regulated clinical trials.

“I think it could be widely used, if it’s proven safe,” said Dr. Paula Amato, a co-author of the study and reproductive endocrinologist at O.H.S.U. Besides creating more healthy embryos for in vitro fertilization, she said, it could be used when screening embryos is not an option or to reduce arduous IVF cycles for women.

Dr. Mitalipov has pushed the scientific envelope before, generating ethical controversy with a so-called three-parent baby procedure that would place the nucleus of the egg of a woman with defective cellular mitochondria into the egg from a healthy woman. The F.D.A. has not approved trials of the method, but Britain may begin one soon.

The new study involves hypertrophic cardiomyopathy, a disease affecting about one in 500 people, which can cause sudden heart failure, often in young athletes.

It is caused by a mutation in a gene called MYBPC3. If one parent has a mutated copy, there is a 50 percent chance of passing the disease to children.

Using sperm from a man with hypertrophic cardiomyopathy and eggs from 12 healthy women, the researchers created fertilized eggs. Injecting CRISPR-Cas9, which works as a genetic scissors, they snipped out the mutated DNA sequence on the male MYBPC3 gene.

They injected a synthetic healthy DNA sequence into the fertilized egg, expecting that the male genome would copy that sequence into the cut portion. That is how this gene-editing process works in other cells in the body, and in mouse embryos, Dr. Mitalipov said.

Instead, the male gene copied the healthy sequence from the female gene. The authors don't know why it happened.

Maybe human sex cells or gametes evolved to repair themselves because they are the only cells that transmit genes to offspring and "need special protection," said Juan Carlos Izpisua Belmonte, a co-author and geneticist at the Salk Institute.

Out of 54 embryos, 36 emerged mutation-free, a significant improvement over natural circumstances in which about half would not have the mutation. Another 13 embryos also emerged without the mutation, but not in every cell.

The researchers tried to eliminate the problem by acting at an earlier stage, injecting the egg with the sperm and CRISPR-Cas9 simultaneously, instead of waiting to inject CRISPR-Cas9 into the already fertilized egg.

That resulted in 42 of 58 embryos, 72 percent, with two mutation-free copies of the gene in every cell. They also found no unwanted mutations in the embryos, which were destroyed after about three days.

The method was not perfect. The remaining 16 embryos had unwanted additions or deletions of DNA. Dr. Mitalipov said he believed fine-tuning the process would make at least 90 percent of embryos mutation-free.

And for disease-causing mutations on maternal genes, the same process should occur, with the father's healthy genetic sequence being copied, he said.

But the technique will not work if both parents have two defective copies. Then, scientists would have to determine how to coax one gene to copy a synthetic DNA sequence, Dr. Mitalipov said.

Otherwise, he said, it should work with many diseases, "a variety of different heritable mutations."

R. Alta Charo, a bioethicist at University of Wisconsin at Madison, who led the committee with Dr. Hynes, said the new discovery could also yield more information about causes of infertility and miscarriages.

She doubts a flood of couples will have "edited children."

"Nobody's going to do this for trivial reasons," Dr. Charo said. "Sex is cheaper and it's more fun than IVF, so unless you've got a real need, you're not going to use it."

CHAPTER 5

Smart Homes and the Internet of Things

The Internet of Things is an integrated network of tools and technology designed to enhance people's lives to create a Smart Home that can be managed, monitored, and adapted by voice, apps or online. Lights can be turned off by phone. The contents of a refrigerator can be seen through an app while shopping. A thermostat adapts to changing outdoor conditions to keep a constant indoor temperature. While many people enjoy the conveniences that Smart Home integration provides, some are concerned about the vast amount of data that device companies are now able to collect.

Thinking of Rigging Your Home With Smart Devices? Start Here

BY DAMON DARLIN | MARCH 8, 2017

SHOPPING FOR consumer electronics can be overwhelming. The staff of the The Wirecutter and The Sweethome, product review websites owned by The New York Times Company, do the hard work of narrowing down the options. We spoke with Grant Clauser, smart home editor at The Wirecutter, about how to sort through the choices for home automation.

Q. *How do I get started rigging my home to work for me?*

A. There are two kinds of smart-home people: those who want specific gadgets to solve particular problems and those who envision a totally integrated smart home.

Most people fall into the first category, so they should think about what problem they want to solve or what daily task they want to simplify. If they want to adjust their kitchen lights from bed, then get a smart light switch or bulbs. If they want to know who's at the front door when they're away, then get a smart video doorbell. Eventually that person may want to add another device (rigging a smart home can get addictive, I can assure you), and at that point I'd tell the person to weigh the benefits of adding something designed to work with the first device versus something that will remain completely independent.

People in the second category, who plan to go all-in for the smart home, should probably start with an overall control system. Instead of a collection of gadgets, you are going for a system that gets them to all work together. This usually means a hub like SmartThings or Wink. These hubs work with the most popular wireless protocols (Z-Wave being the primary one), and allow users to pick from a wide assortment of compatible devices. The planning and programming phase may take some time and is best for people who like to tinker, test and try out new things.

A lot of people already have bits of home automation: a Nest thermostat, a web-connected surveillance camera, an Amazon Echo.

Q. *Do they have to worry something they own won't work with another they just bought?*

A. Your first purchases may influence subsequent buying decisions. Having devices that work together is convenient, especially if you have a lot of devices, but if you have only a few and are comfortable opening a separate app for your smart smoke alarm and another for your smart water sensor, you'll be O.K.

There's really nothing wrong with having a Wi-Fi camera and a Wi-Fi thermostat that don't communicate with each other. You may, however, be missing out on some features if they don't. For instance, if your thermostat and camera work together, the geofencing built into your camera can trigger your thermostat to adjust the temperature when you leave the house. That might be a function you value.

Q. *What products make no sense to you?*

A. My own rule, which I'll probably break eventually, is that if I need to be in front of the device to take advantage of its primary use, then I don't need it to be smart. A lot of kitchen gadgets fall under this category. There's not much to be gained from an internet-connected toaster or internet-connected coffee maker because I need to be in the room with it to grab the toast or coffee, anyway.

Q. *What have you done in your own house?*

A. My house is a work in progress. I'm always pulling out some device and adding another.

At one point I had seven home security systems running. Most of my lights can be controlled through Amazon Alexa devices, either via smart switches or smart bulbs. When I go to bed I can shut off the downstairs lights, confirm that the thermostat has gone into night mode and lock the front door, all with my phone. My home theater system — yes, I put in one of those, too — is integrated through a universal remote and hub, which also controls the room's lights, and all that can be operated by voice through an Echo Dot. To watch a movie all I have to do is say "Alexa, turn on Netflix," and the projector turns on, the system loads up Netflix and the lights automatically turn off. All of that is done with easy D.I.Y. products.

Q. *Is there anything you can't live without?*

A. My Amazon Echo and Dots are probably the things I use the most. They're connected to my lights, run my home theater, keep my shopping lists, read me the morning news and play music. I'd really miss those if they were gone.

Q. *What's your next home project?*

A. I just ordered some motion sensors for my Hue lights so my lights will automatically turn on when someone walks in the room. That will probably annoy my family for a while.

3 Gadgets You Didn't Know You Needed, but Are Worth Buying

BY ANN-MARIE ALCÁNTARA | APRIL 24, 2018

IT'S EASY TO FORGET how far technology has come in just a few years. We went from praying that our CD players wouldn't skip to streaming music wirelessly to wearing AirPods in our ears. But even some recent devices have made the jump from high-end items for tech enthusiasts to must-haves for many homes. Here are a few of them.

VOICE-ACTIVATED ASSISTANTS

"Weird." "Curious." "Baffling." "Quite Stupid." These words all once described Alexa, the voice-activated digital assistant on Amazon's Echo device. But Amazon says the Echo Dot, a smaller, less expensive version of the Echo, was its "top-selling device" during the holiday season.

In 2014, it was odd to even consider owning an Echo — and impossible to buy without an invitation from Amazon. Today, you can pick from five Echo models. Or, you can try Google's version: the Google Home, Google Home Mini or Google Home Max. Apple has also released a digital assistant device, the HomePod, which is fully capable with Siri. You can have your pick of digital assistants — each with varying capabilities of improving your life.

Alexa now has more than 15,000 skills, meaning any Echo device can go beyond describing the weather or playing music. The Google Assistant, first released in 2016, is catching up.

So why buy one now? First, they're relatively inexpensive and far easier to use and understand than they were when first released. Think back to MP3 players or early smartphones: People learned a lot about using the products and became so adjusted to them that they didn't know how to go back. Second, the future is paved with smart home devices, and voice-activated assistants to control them are becoming

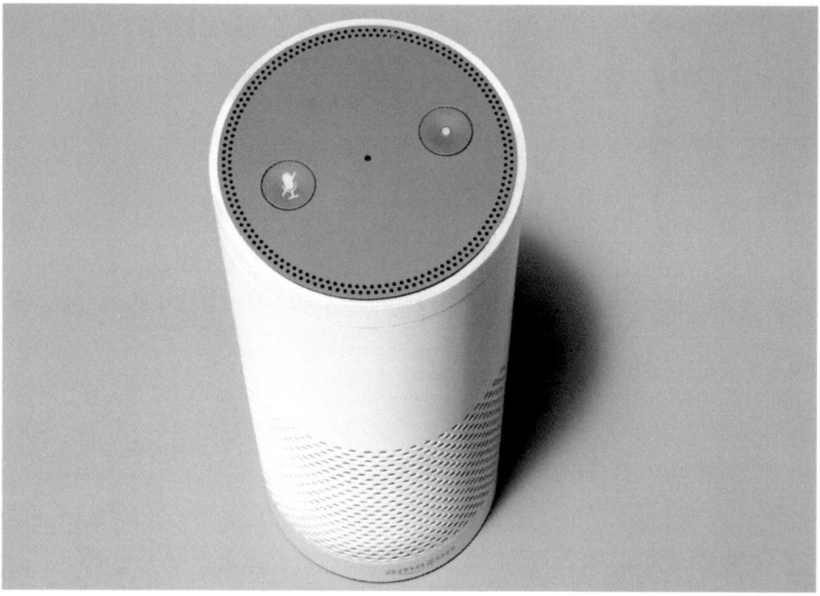

JENS MORTENSEN FOR THE NEW YORK TIMES

The Amazon Echo.

ubiquitous. The Echo and Google Home are no longer "test products" — the companies behind them want them to last.

ROKU

Prepare to feel either really old or really young: Roku players have existed for 10 years. The first Roku player streamed Netflix (and only Netflix) to your TV. Now, you have your pick of streaming devices, from Chromecast to Apple TV to a variety of Roku players. If you don't have one, it's about time you invested in one. Several devices are budget-friendly and portable. I f you're all about video quality and immersive audio, there are options that deliver.

When many of these devices were first introduced, they could stream only certain services. When Google first offered the Chromecast in 2013, it could support only Netflix and YouTube. Now, it works with Hulu, HBO Go, the CW, Sling, VUDU and hundreds more.

Wirecutter, a New York Times company, recommends the Roku

Streaming Stick+, which retails for about $65. It comes with an external Wi-Fi antenna, lots of supported streaming content (including 4K video), and a customizable home screen so you can go straight to the services you use. Best of all, you can take it with you on vacation or a business trip.

Of course, there are cheaper options, like the Roku Streaming Stick for $45 or Google's Chromecast, for $35. The point, of course, is to finally embrace lying on the couch, binge-watching your next new favorite show.

BLUETOOTH TRACKER

The gadget that finds all your lost gadgets.

In 2013, a small company started a crowdfunding campaign, met its goal, racked up more than 200,000 presales and earned a loyal customer base. Today that company, Tile, makes a well-known Bluetooth tracker that attaches to anything you deem important and keeps track of it via a mobile app. There are now other Bluetooth trackers that make finding your keys, wallet or anything else easier than ever.

Wirecutter recommends the Tile Sport for its Bluetooth range, alarm volume and handy crowd-finding feature. Basically, if you lose an item that has a Tile attached to it, anyone with the Tile app who passes by will help ping the location of your lost item to you. The person doesn't have to actively use the app to help you (and won't know you lost something).

If you prefer a Bluetooth tracker with a replaceable battery (but less stellar Bluetooth range and no crowd-finding), Wirecutter recommends the TrackR Pixel. You can replace the battery, rather than the whole product, and the alert system includes flashing lights.

So, while you're reminiscing about making a trip to Blockbuster for movies or going through the couch cushions to find your keys, just know that there's a gadget for that now. They aren't perfect, but they do give you one less thing to worry about.

Amazon Buys Ring, Maker of Smart Home Products

BY NICK WINGFIELD | FEB. 27, 2018

AMAZON SAID TUESDAY that it had acquired Ring, a maker of internet-connected doorbells and cameras, pushing more deeply into the home security market.

The deal is worth around $1.1 billion, according to a person briefed on the deal who would speak only anonymously because the terms were private.

Ring is best known for a doorbell with a security camera inside. The device allows homeowners to monitor visitors at their front door through an app on their phone, even if they're not at home. Amazon has made home automation a major focus because of the success of its Echo family of products, which allow users to control thermostats, surveillance cameras and other connected devices using voice commands.

Amazon's Echo Spot device already works with Ring doorbells, allowing people to look at footage from the cameras on the Echo Spot's screen. Amazon had invested an undisclosed amount in Ring through its Alexa Fund, which finances start-ups that integrate their products with Alexa, the Amazon intelligent assistant that powers Echoes and other devices.

Buying Ring, though, suggests that Amazon has more ambitious plans for the product than it could achieve through a partnership.

Luke Schoenfelder, chief executive of Latch, a start-up that makes a family of smart locks, said he believed that Amazon would make a more serious effort to enter the home security market and compete against companies like ADT, Comcast and Alarm.com. Mr. Schoenfelder speculated that Amazon could seek to make home security part of its Prime membership service, which today includes free and fast delivery of orders and video streaming.

“You could imagine some kind of bundled offering with Ring’s capabilities,” he said.

ADT’s stock fell sharply after the deal became public on Tuesday afternoon. It ended the day down 4.6 percent.

The companies declined to say much about their plans. “Ring’s home security products and services have delighted customers since Day 1,” Amazon said in a statement. “We’re excited to work with this talented team and help them in their mission to keep homes safe and secure.”

Ring’s statement said: “We’ll be able to achieve even more by partnering with an inventive, customer-centric company like Amazon. We look forward to being a part of the Amazon team as we work toward our vision for safer neighborhoods.”

Ring’s internet doorbells start at $179. People who want to use them to record video must pay for that capability, with plans starting at $3 a month or $30 a year. The company also makes stand-alone security cameras.

Amazon has taken some baby steps into home security. Last year it began selling an indoor security camera of its own design, Amazon Cloud Cam, and in December it acquired Blink, a maker of inexpensive internet security cameras and doorbells.

A service called Amazon Key uses cameras and internet-connected door locks to allow delivery people to drop orders inside customers’ homes.

Google, one of Amazon’s biggest rivals, is also an increasingly important player in home automation and security, with its Nest thermostats and security cameras.

James McQuivey, an analyst at Forrester Research, said he believed that Amazon had bought Ring so it could add more intelligent capabilities to its doorbells and cameras, like the ability to use software to recognize faces at the front door.

“I think it’s about going to the next level and having Alexa say, ‘James, your fifth grader just walked in, and I locked the door behind them,’ ” he said. “It’s where these technologies have to go.”

Is My Not-So-Smart House Watching Me?

BY RONDA KAYSEN | APRIL 27, 2018

MY LIGHT BULBS sometimes go rogue.

Invariably, this happens at some inopportune moment, like at midnight, when I walk into my bedroom and discover that to turn on the lights, I first need to install a software update to an app on my iPhone.

The porch light periodically misbehaves, too, refusing to automatically turn on, despite the schedule I diligently added to that same app. I could flip the switch like normal people do, but what would be the fun in that? These lights are supposed to be Smart, with a capital S, responding to my whim as all Smart things do.

If I wanted to get super smart, I could connect the bulbs to an Amazon Echo and shout at Alexa, commanding her to flood my room with light, or dim it to a sultry glow whenever the mood strikes.

Of course, there's a chance she might feel lonely, and randomly decide to talk about the weather, as she does in the middle of the night with Sarah Coffey, an editor for Dow Jones Newswires, who lives in Maplewood, N.J. "I don't understand why Alexa is speaking to me at 3 in the morning," Ms. Coffey, 44, said. But she is.

We could blame Ms. Coffey's husband, Ben Berkowitz, 39, a vice president for digital at WNBC in New York, for turning the family's home into a techie wonderland. Along with that Echo, the family has Google Home, digital home security, a lock with keyless entry, and a Nest thermostat that insists on keeping the internal temperature at a crisp 62 degrees even when people are home.

Ms. Coffey has so many apps on her phone monitoring her home that she has lost track of all the things they do. "I appreciate his efforts to computerize our house," she said of Mr. Berkowitz. "I just wish I could turn on a light without having to ask my phone to do it."

For as long as we've been imagining the wonders of household

JULIETTE BORDA

gadgets, we've been struggling with them. No sooner did Americans have TVs in their homes than Zenith invented a remote control, calling it Lazy Bones, in 1950. These little rectangular boxes were intended to make our leisure time more leisurely, but as they have become commonplace, they have contributed to our growing waistlines and marital discord (except, of course, when they are lost in the couch cushions).

Even the Jetsons, the fabulously futuristic cartoon characters from the early 1960s, struggled with their digital devices, as automatic bed ejectors, digital breakfast makers and robotic toothbrushes caused more chaos than convenience in the cartoon's first episode.

Yet our love affair with stuff smarter than us continues. Roughly a third of United States households already have smart gadgets, and by 2022, more than half of all households will, according to the research firm Statista.

Light bulbs are just the beginning. I could get a Colgate Connect toothbrush to map my mouth and give me pointers; a Roomba vacuuming robot to clean up after me; or a smart refrigerator to warn me that the milk might curdle. I could swap out my doorbell for one with a camera, delivering me live footage of the UPS driver dropping off a Bluetooth-enabled Instant Pot that can monitor how quickly the rice cooks.

All those sleek boxes and digital keypads carry the promise that, with just one more purchase and a swipe right, our lives will be easier, and our homes will run more smoothly. When we are at home, "our desires are right up front and we want those desires satisfied," said Paul Levinson, a professor of communication and media studies at Fordham University and the author of "New New Media." "That is the basis for all these things that we have in the house."

Would my life be easier if I could keep track of dinner on my iPhone? I don't know. But it probably would be more monitored. Even as we are in the midst of a collective freakout about the data that Facebook has been gathering and sharing without our permission, many of us are busily installing equipment that potentially bugs our homes and tracks our movements, conversations and routines.

"Pretty much anything that I say in my living room could be recorded and could be transferred somewhere else," said Craig A. Shue, an associate professor of computer science at Worcester Polytechnic Institute, referring to devices with speakers and microphones like Google Home and Amazon Echo. "The risks are substantial."

Last December, a Gizmodo reporter turned her one-bedroom San Francisco apartment into a smart home, connecting as many appliances and belongings to the internet as possible, including her mattress and coffee maker. While she found the experience mostly annoying, another reporter kept tabs on all the data that left her apartment. Not a single hour went by when her router was quiet — at all times, at least one gadget was communicating with its home server.

All that data mining has given some Americans pause. Seventy percent of consumers worry that hackers might access their smart devices at home, and 58 percent fear a lack of privacy from manufacturers that have access to their data, conversations, voice patterns and search history, according to iQor, a customer service outsourcing provider.

But anxiety alone hasn't been a deterrent, since we keep buying the stuff. We rationalize this uncomfortable truth because smart technology does have the potential to make life easier and, perhaps, safer.

Affix a smart sensor to your water heater and you could be alerted to an impending flood. Install a smart lock on your door and you could remotely let a neighbor in to feed the cat, or get an alert at the office when your teenager gets home from school.

As for me, I live in an old house with few overhead light fixtures. It seems like a banal problem, but filling my bedroom with lamps that turn on with an iPhone means I don't have to call an electrician to drill holes in my ceiling and walls to install permanent lighting. I certainly enjoy the convenience, and savings, even if it means I have yet another reason to stare at my phone.

To Invade Homes, Tech Is Trying to Get in Your Kitchen

BY BRIAN X. CHEN | MARCH 25, 2018

SAN FRANCISCO — On a recent Saturday night, German Salazar made chicken tacos for his friends while they chatted with him in his kitchen. Occasionally, he interrupted the conversation to talk to another friend: Google.

Mr. Salazar was speaking to Google Home, the artificially intelligent speaker living on his kitchen counter. "Hey Google, set a timer for 20 minutes," he said, to activate a countdown for when the chicken would be cooked and ready for shredding.

At first, Mr. Salazar's friends snickered when he talked to the speaker. But after a few bottles of wine, everyone began grilling Google Home with questions and requests: "How much did Jamie Lee Curtis make in 'True Lies'?" and "Tell me a joke."

For many people, the kitchen is the center of the home and a locus for interactions that go beyond preparing and eating food. Now tech companies and appliance makers, aiming to deepen their relationships with customers, are increasingly targeting the room that is synonymous with togetherness.

Household brands like Whirlpool, Samsung and Bosch are racing against tech behemoths like Google and Amazon to dominate the kitchen with internet-connected appliances and cooking gadgets that include refrigerators embedded with touch screens, smart dishwashers and connected countertop screens with artificially intelligent assistants that react to spoken commands.

Yet the so-called smart kitchen remains a tough sell. With the kitchen often a hub for families and friends, habits there can be hard to change. And many people see the kitchen and mealtimes as a haven from their otherwise always-connected lifestyle. Only 5 percent of American households own smart appliances today, up from 3 percent

CHRIS PHILPOT

in 2014, according to the research firm Parks Associates.

"Will we see a reinvention of the kitchen like we saw in the living room?" said Michael Wolf, a tech analyst who hosts a podcast and a conference about the smart kitchen. "I don't think it will happen overnight. There's going to be a lot of skepticism."

Apart from their fears of disrupting the rhythms and patterns in the heart of the home, people may be hesitant to incorporate smart devices into their kitchens because of the costs of maintaining such appliances, which are often difficult to repair and use expensive components like touch screens. They also may worry about longevity: A touch-screen refrigerator may look modern today, but who knows how dated it may appear in five years?

And with many smart kitchen appliances incorporating internet connections, cameras or microphones, digital privacy has become a concern. Security researchers said that one problem with smart appliances is that, unlike tech companies, household brands lack the cybersecurity expertise to vet products for vulnerabilities.

Julie Kim-Whinston had some of those misgivings when she renovated her San Francisco home recently. For the revamped kitchen, she bought appliances from Wolf, Viking and Bosch — all lacking big screens, virtual assistants or internet connections. Ms. Kim-Whinston, a consultant in outerwear and sportswear, said she found smart appliances unappealing because the tech components could quickly go obsolete.

The kitchen and the dining area are also where she, her husband and their two sons, ages 5 and 7, congregate and converse, she said. She said she did not want her children to be exposed to a refrigerator with a big touch screen.

"Knowing how addictive their personalities are, they would literally stare at the refrigerator screen hoping for something to come up," she said. "They'd be touching it and moving it, hoping it's a video game."

But the potential payoff for manufacturers makes the kitchen an enticing target. The global kitchen appliances market is expected to balloon to $253.4 billion by 2020, up from about $175 billion in 2014, according to Allied Market Research.

That has companies spreading their tech tentacles into kitchens with a variety of approaches. Samsung, the No. 1 phone maker that popularized smartphones with extra-large screens, this year unveiled a new version of Family Hub, a smart refrigerator that understands voice commands and sports a 21.5-inch touch screen. The appliance has three built-in cameras, which can beam live images of the fridge's contents to a phone.

Samsung bills the fridge as the next control center for a home — albeit a pricey one. Family Hub refrigerators start at about $3,500.

"We'd really like consumers, at some point of time, to look back and say, 'These days, a refrigerator without a screen feels awkward,' " said Sunggy Koo, Samsung's vice president for smart appliances.

Samsung's aim is for people to someday conduct their digital lives with equal ease from a fridge, a phone, a television or a car. Fed by data about you in the cloud — and with the help of a virtual assistant — all of the machines will operate in perfect synchrony to enable a maximally efficient domestic life.

Bosch is taking a more conservative approach. Its smart dishwashers, ovens and coffee machines, which range in price from about $1,300 to $3,100, look just like their disconnected counterparts and mostly use their internet connections for remote diagnostics. If a problem occurs, the appliance can automatically send an error code to Bosch's customer service team, which can help determine whether you should fix the problem yourself or schedule a repair.

"Whenever we talk to our customers, we get the feedback that they really appreciate technology when it makes their life simple, but they don't want to bother with additional complexity," said Anja Prescher, Bosch's director of brand marketing.

Whirlpool emphasizes the use of smartphones as kitchen companions. The company last year acquired Yummly, a recipe site that developed an app for scanning items in a refrigerator or pantry. The app then comes up with suggestions for what to cook and walks the user through recipes.

For now, Amazon and Google are having some of the most notable successes in the kitchen, even though their devices are not specific to that room. Many people use Amazon's Echo speaker or Google Home, both of which are embedded with the companies' smart virtual assistants, for setting kitchen timers or looking up recipes.

To take advantage of the frequency with which these devices end up in kitchens, the companies are expanding on those products with voice-controlled smart screens. Last year, Amazon debuted Echo Show, which can load step-by-step recipes on the screen. Google this year unveiled Smart Display, a software system that it shares with manufacturers like Lenovo, which will release smart screens this year that feature Google Assistant and can run apps and play recipe videos.

But those devices have also raised privacy questions. The Amazon and Google screens constantly listen for voice commands, and they include cameras for placing video calls. Amazon and Google said they offer the ability to mute the microphones and turn the cameras off.

Richard Gunther, a software consultant who works from home in

Annapolis, Md., hates cooking but loves kitchen gadgets and high-end appliances. He uses his Amazon Echo to turn on his sous-vide cooker and he also owns a $399 Tovala smart oven, which includes a bar code scanner to identify meal kits and set the proper cooking time and temperature.

Yet Mr. Gunther isn't sold on the brave new world of smart appliances. He said that when he was shopping for a new refrigerator late last year, he researched Samsung's Family Hub and was turned off by the idea of using cameras to look at what food was inside. Why not just open the door and check?

"Trying to keep track of whatever I have inside by remembering to scan something or put the milk carton back in the same place where I had it before and not have it obscured by a piece of fruit in front of it?" he said. "I can't be bothered by all of that."

He ended up with a dumb fridge from Sub-Zero for $23,000.

From Westworld to Best World for the Internet of Things

OPINION | BY JONATHAN ZITTRAIN | JUNE 3, 2018

LAST MONTH THE F.B.I. issued an urgent warning: Everyone with home internet routers should reboot them to shed them of malware from "foreign cyberactors."

Putting aside the strangeness that for once power-cycling a device could perform an effective exorcism upon it, the episode reveals more than just the potential for disruption of internet access for people using equipment they never expect to have to physically manage. It also underscores how unprepared we are to manage downstream-networked devices and appliances — the "internet of things" — that are vulnerable to attack.

A longstanding ethos of internet development lets anyone build and share new code and services, with consequences to be dealt with later. I call this the "procrastination principle," and I don't regret supporting it. But it's hard to feel the same way about the internet of things.

Worries about security for these devices have become widespread, and they fall roughly into two categories.

First, compromised networked things can endanger their users. In 2015, Chrysler recalled 1.4 million vehicles after researchers showed they could hack a Jeep and disable its brakes and transmission. Coffee makers and other appliances with heating elements could have safety features overridden, starting a fire. And an alert was issued on certain pacemakers last year after vulnerabilities were found that could allow attackers to gain unauthorized access and issue commands to the devices.

Second, hacking even a tiny subset of the 10 billion and counting networked things can produce threats larger than any one consumer. Individually these devices may be too small to care about; together they become too big to fail. Security systems in a city could be made to sound an alarm simultaneously. Light bulbs can be organized into bot armies, directed to harm any other internet-connected target. And worse than a single Jeep executing an unexpected sharp left turn is a whole fleet of them doing so.

Short of rejecting internet integration with appliances, dealing with this is not easy. As with home routers, we tend to keep appliances around for years, so vulnerabilities aren't phased out quickly.

In fact, many vendors might stop issuing firmware updates for physical objects even while they're still widely in use — abandoning the public to problems lurking in embedded code. And otherwise-valuable "over the air" security updates could also be a gateway to a hack, especially for small vendors of cheap if useful objects like $5 drones.

The unusual problems of the internet of things call for unusual solutions.

The first confronts the life-cycle problem. Companies making a critical mass of internet-enabled products should be required to post a "networked safety bond" to be cashed in if they abandon maintenance for a product, or fold entirely. Insurers can price bonds according to companies' security practices. There's an example of such a system for coal mining, to provide for reclamation and cleanup should the mining company leave behind a wasteland.

For internet-connected appliances, "reclamation" can entail work by nonprofit foundations to maintain the code for abandoned products, creating an "island of misfit toys," in the parlance of the famed 1964 Rankin/Bass stop-motion Christmas special. Proceeds from redeemed bonds would go to these foundations to maintain the products, like the way the Mozilla Foundation has transformed the 1998 Netscape browser long after its originators left the scene.

A second intervention would require networked products modeled after analog counterparts to work even without connectivity. A smart coffee maker shouldn't be so clever that it can't make coffee without internet access. Switchover to non-connectivity mode will not merely help prevent things from becoming useless when the internet goes down, or if the original vendor disappears or jacks up service prices. It can also provide a soft landing for appliances that reach the end of their supported life cycles while still beloved by owners.

Finally, networked devices made by different vendors need to be able to communicate with one another — the way that, say, Mac and PC users seamlessly exchange email. That prevents a household from becoming locked into a single vendor for all its appliances. It also prevents us from flocking to one or two vendors whose compromise could cause widespread consequences.

While procrastination around security has been vital to the expansion of the internet, "later" doesn't mean "never." We can create incentives to design networked devices for both interoperability and safety, and to plan for remediation when some things inevitably go wrong. We can enjoy the best rather than worst of both worlds.

JONATHAN ZITTRAIN (@ZITTRAIN) IS A PROFESSOR OF INTERNATIONAL LAW AND OF COMPUTER SCIENCE AT HARVARD, A CO-FOUNDER OF THE BERKMAN KLEIN CENTER FOR INTERNET & SOCIETY AND THE AUTHOR OF "THE FUTURE OF THE INTERNET — AND HOW TO STOP IT."

Looking Beyond the Internet of Things

BY QUENTIN HARDY | JAN. 1, 2016

SAN FRANCISCO — If you have sent email on Google or used Microsoft's browser or databases, you have touched the technology handiwork of Adam Bosworth.

Mr. Bosworth, a tall and grizzled but still trim 60-year-old, is a Johnny Appleseed of sorts in the tech industry, with a penchant for being intimately involved in the creation of generations of widely used technology.

While it is never easy to predict what the next big thing will be, identifying what Mr. Bosworth is working on is always good for clues. Right now, along with competitors at companies like Amazon and Google, he is building what some call a "data singularity."

Imagine if almost everything — streets, car bumpers, doors, hydroelectric dams — had a tiny sensor. That is already happening through so-called Internet-of-Things projects run by big companies like General Electric and IBM.

All those devices and sensors would also wirelessly connect to far-off data centers, where millions of computer servers manage and learn from all that information.

Those servers would then send back commands to help whatever the sensors are connected to operate more effectively: A home automatically turns up the heat ahead of cold weather moving in, or streetlights behave differently when traffic gets bad. Or imagine an insurance company instantly resolving who has to pay for what an instant after a fender-bender because it has been automatically fed information about the accident.

Think of it as one, enormous process in which machines gather information, learn and change based on what they learn. All in seconds.

"I'm interested in affecting five billion people," said Mr. Bosworth, a former star at Microsoft and Google who now makes interactive

JASON HENRY FOR THE NEW YORK TIMES

Adam Bosworth at the Salesforce office in San Francisco.

software at Salesforce.com, an online software company that runs sales for thousands of corporations. "We're headed into one of those historic discontinuities where society changes."

It is lofty language, no doubt, but he and others believe they are on the brink of one of the next big shifts in computing, perhaps as big as the web browser or the personal computer.

But building an automated system that can react to all that data like a thoughtful person is fiendishly hard — and that may be Mr. Bosworth's last great challenge to solve.

It is difficult to say just how big this business could be, but there are two good indicators: Analysts at Gartner estimate that by 2019 retail cloud computing — the data center side of the equation Mr. Bosworth is working on — will double in size, to $314 billion. The sensors on objects will be a $2.6 trillion business, an increase of 250 percent, Gartner estimates.

Mr. Bosworth went to Harvard with Bill Gates, where he took just one class in computers while studying Asian history. He nonetheless landed a job on Wall Street, where he persuaded his bosses to give him $1 million for minicomputers — the cutting edge of computing before personal computers — that could deliver the first instant reports on how business was doing.

He got interested in tech's next big thing, PCs, and wrote an early spreadsheet program. He joined Microsoft in 1989. His first years there were spent on databases, but as the Internet got big he helped turn browsers from software that looks up web pages to software that interacts with the web.

He and Mr. Gates repeatedly argued over the importance of the Internet, according to people there at the time. Mr. Gates may also have goaded Mr. Bosworth, knowing he is the sort who does not like to be told something is not possible.

"He sees out into the future, but not too far that you can't build something," said Brad Silverberg, a Seattle venture capitalist who has known Mr. Bosworth since 1981 and was his boss at Microsoft. "If you want to make sure something gets done, tell him not to do it."

The son of a demanding private school headmaster, Mr. Bosworth also clashed with Larry Page, Google's co-founder and chief executive, while working there on interactive software and a failed effort to build online health services.

"We had styles that weren't synergistic," said Mr. Bosworth. "He looks intensively at massive amounts of data-gathering, and assumes he'll be able to do something with it using math. I was focused on getting people to communicate with other people."

He left Google in 2007 to start Keas, an online health management company. He left in 2011 for Salesforce, but is still on Keas's board.

Marc Benioff, the chief executive at Salesforce and a friend of Mr. Bosworth, asked him to look at the technology being used at the San Francisco company, which was founded in 1999 and was one of the first to use cloud computing technology.

Over lunch a few months later, Mr. Bosworth told Mr. Benioff that his once-revolutionary company was in peril.

"Computers are 50 times faster than when Salesforce started," he said. "I told Marc, 'There is a whole new technology that is going to overtake you, the way the web overtook Microsoft.' "

That technology — the data singularity — is what Mr. Bosworth is now working on at Salesforce.

If he is right, this new era in computing will have effects far beyond a little more efficiency. Consumers could see a vast increase in the number of services, ads and product upgrades that are sold alongside most goods. And products that respond to their owner's tastes — something already seen in smartphone upgrades, connected cars from BMW or Tesla, or entertainment devices like the Amazon Echo — could change product design.

Analysts foresee a scramble to own and manage these systems and their data, and ever more power accruing to just a few companies like Google, Amazon and Microsoft, which already have the global computing systems and reach to make it happen.

"The idea is turning the world into a smart object that can be continuously improved, and we couldn't be more excited," said Matthew Wood, the general manager of product strategy at Amazon Web Services, or A.W.S., the retailer's giant cloud computing business.

Few outfits have the engineering talent to manage this sort of thing. One year after starting the business, for example, Microsoft's cloud handles a trillion sensor messages a week.

Salesforce, which is worth $54 billion, is an underdog compared to that tiny group of tech behemoths. It lacks global data centers, but does control important data, like information about what customers are buying.

Who will ultimately control that data, from the sensors to the cloud and back, is one of the most contentious questions in tech.

"You've got Amazon knowing everything about purchasing, Google knowing everything about what people do on the Internet, and Salesforce knowing everything about the revenue side of a business," said Scott Raney, a venture capitalist at Redpoint Ventures who invests in companies related to what Mr. Bosworth is working on.

"Lay computer processing on all that, and it's powerful to a point where a little creepiness sets in; no one else will have the data," he added. "I'm buying the stock of all the companies. I just hope they'll be benevolent dictators."

Glossary

autonomous car Self-driving car.

blockchain A digital ledger that can record any transaction of value.

car-service A type of business that provides their customers with rides from one place to another.

Crispr Acronym for Clustered Regularly Interspaced Short Palindromic Repeats, it is a series of short repeating DNA sequences that bacteria use to identify specific viruses that attack them.

cryptocurrency A digital form of exchange that uses a decentralized system to record transactions and manage the issuing of new units, and cryptography to secure the transactions.

database A collection of information stored in a computer.

entrepreneur Someone who runs their own business.

eugenics Selective breeding in humans.

genome The complete set of DNA of an organism.

hands-free A device or app which can be operated by a user without their hands.

home sharing An arrangement where unrelated people share a living space.

innovation The process of creating and introduction new ideas, technology, and ways of doing things.

investment Purchasing something (shares, property, etc.) with the intention of making a profit from it.

landlord A person who rents out land or buildings they own.

lawsuit A claim that is taken to court to be settled.

legislation A collection of laws relating a specific subject.

lodging taxes Taxes on the rental of accommodation.

municipal To do with a town or district.

patent A right granted to a person who has invented a product or a process that for a limited period of time prevents other people from making, using or selling the same product or process.

regulators Members of government responsible for the development and enforcement of laws.

residential Areas and places designated for people to live in.

ride-sharing An arrangement where one or more unrelated people are driven from one place to another by a vehicle owner.

shares Units of ownership in a company.

sharing economy A system where individuals provide services to one another without being employed by larger organizations.

Silicon Valley A region in the San Francisco Bay Area known as a hub for technology and start-up companies.

start-up A new company that is still growing.

subpoena A legal order for a person or organization to attend court proceedings.

surge pricing A system where prices for a service change based on current demand.

tenant A person or organization which rents land or buildings from a landlord.

valuation An estimate of how much something is worth.

Media Literacy Terms

"Media literacy" refers to the ability to access, understand, critically assess and create media. The following terms are important components of media literacy, and they will help you critically engage with the articles in this title.

attribution The method by which a source is identified or by which facts and information are assigned to the person who provided them.

balance Principle of journalism that both perspectives of an argument should be presented in a fair way.

bias A disposition of prejudice in favor of a certain idea, person or perspective.

byline Name of the writer, usually placed between the headline and the story.

caption Identifying copy for a picture; also called a legend or cutline.

column Type of story that is a regular feature, often on a recurring topic, written by the same journalist, generally known as a columnist.

credibility The quality of being trustworthy and believable, said of a journalistic source.

feature story Article designed to entertain as well as to inform.

headline Type, usually 18 point or larger, used to introduce a story.

impartiality Principle of journalism that a story should not reflect a journalist's bias and should contain balance.

intention The motive or reason behind something, such as the publication of a news story.

news story An article or style of expository writing that reports news, generally in a straightforward fashion and without editorial comment.

op-ed An opinion piece that reflects a prominent journalist's opinion on topic of interest.

paraphrase The summary of an individual's words, with attribution, rather than a direct quotation of their exact words.

quotation The use of an individual's exact words indicated by the use of quotation marks and proper attribution.

reliability The quality of being dependable and accurate, said of a journalistic source.

rhetorical device Technique in writing intending to persuade the reader or communicate a message from a certain perspective.

source The origin of the information reported in journalism.

style A distinctive use of language in writing or speech; also a news or publishing organization's rules for consistent use of language with regards to spelling, punctuation, typography and capitalization, usually regimented by a house style guide.

tone A manner of expression in writing or speech.

Media Literacy Questions

1. Identify the various sources cited in the article "Businesses Turn to Airbnb" (on page 24). How does the journalist attribute information to each of these sources in his article? How effective are his attributions in helping the reader identify his sources?

2. In "Falcon Heavy, in a Roar of Thunder, Carries SpaceX's Ambition Into Orbit" (on page 94), Kenneth Chang directly quotes Elon Musk. What are the strengths of the use of a direct quote as opposed to a paraphrase? What are its weaknesses?

3. Compare the headlines of "What Is Bitcoin and How Does It Work?" (on page 110) and "Speed Bumps on the Road to Virtual Cash" (on page 100). Which is a more compelling headline, and why? How could the less compelling headline be changed to better draw the reader's interest?

4. What type of story is "A Powerful New Way to Edit DNA" (on page 154)? Can you identify another article in this collection that is the same type of story?

5. Does Brian X. Chen demonstrate the journalistic principle of impartiality in his article "To Invade Homes, Tech Is Trying to Get in Your Kitchen" (on page 196)? If so, how did he do so? If not, what could he have included to make his article more impartial?

6. "Jennifer Doudna, a Pioneer Who Helped Simplify Genome Editing" (on page 160) is an example of an interview. What are the benefits of providing readers with direct quotes of an interviewed subject's speech? Is the subject of an interview always a reliable source?

7. "Kodak's Dubious Cryptocurrency Gamble" (on page 125) features two photographs. What do these photographs add to the article?

8. What is the intention of the article "The Watchamacallit Economy" (on page 46)? How effectively does it achieve its intended purpose?

9. As a news story develops, a journalist's attitude toward the subject may change. Compare "Speed Bumps on the Road to Virtual Cash" (on page 100) and "Bubble or No, This Virtual Currency Is a Lot of Coin in Any Realm" (on page 105), both by Noam Cohen. Did new information discovered between the publication of these two articles change Noam Cohen's perspective?

10. Identify each of the sources in "In Breakthrough, Scientists Edit a Dangerous Mutation From Genes in Human Embryos" (on page 177) as a primary source or a secondary source. Evaluate the reliability and credibility of each sources. How does your evaluation of each source change your perspective on this article?

Citations

All citations in this list are formatted according to the Modern Language Association's (MLA) style guide.

BOOK CITATION

NEW YORK TIMES EDITORIAL STAFF, THE. *Disruptive Innovation: Uber, Airbnb and Other Companies Reshaping the Market.* New York: New York Times Educational Publishing, 2019.

ONLINE ARTICLE CITATIONS

ALCÁNTARA, ANN-MARIE. "3 Gadgets You Didn't Know You Needed, but Are Worth Buying." *The New York Times*, 24 Apr. 2018, www.nytimes.com/2018/04/24/smarter-living/3-gadgets-you-didnt-know-you-needed-roku-echo-alexa-tile.html.

BADGER, EMILY. "Why Even the Hyperloop Probably Wouldn't Change Your Commute Time." *The New York Times*, 10 Aug. 2017, www.nytimes.com/2017/08/10/upshot/why-even-the-hyperloop-probably-wouldnt-change-your-commute-time.html.

BELLAFANTE, GINIA. "What the Sharing Economy Really Delivers: Entitlement." *The New York Times*, 26 Jan. 2018, https://www.nytimes.com/2018/01/26/nyregion/what-the-sharing-economy-really-delivers-entitlement.html.

BELLUCK, PAM. "In Breakthrough, Scientists Edit a Dangerous Mutation From Genes in Human Embryos." *The New York Times*, 2 Aug. 2017, www.nytimes.com/2017/08/02/science/gene-editing-human-embryos.html.

BRUSTEIN, JOSHUA. "The Smartphone Way to Beckon a Car." *The New York Times*, 16 May 2011, https://www.nytimes.com/2011/05/15/nyregion/uber-and-weeels-offer-car-services-by-phone-app.html.

CARDWELL, DIANE. "Solar Experiment Lets Neighbors Trade Energy Among Themselves." *The New York Times*, 13 Mar. 2017, www.nytimes.com/2017/03/13/business/energy-environment/brooklyn-solar-grid-energy-trading.html.

CHANG, KENNETH. "Falcon Heavy, in a Roar of Thunder, Carries SpaceX's Ambition Into Orbit." *The New York Times*, 6 Feb. 2018, www.nytimes.com/2018/02/06/science/falcon-heavy-spacex-launch.html.

CHEN, BRIAN X. "To Invade Homes, Tech Is Trying to Get in Your Kitchen." *The New York Times*, 25 Mar. 2018, www.nytimes.com/2018/03/25/technology/smart-homes-tech-kitchen.html.

COHEN, NOAM. "Bubble or No, Virtual Bitcoins Show Real Worth." *The New York Times*, 7 Apr. 2013, www.nytimes.com/2013/04/08/business/media/bubble-or-no-virtual-bitcoins-show-real-worth.html.

COHEN, NOAM. "Speed Bumps on the Road to Virtual Cash." *The New York Times*, 3 July 2011, www.nytimes.com/2011/07/04/business/media/04link.html.

COWEN, TYLER. "In an Uber World, Fortune Favors the Freelancer." *The New York Times*, 27 June 2015, www.nytimes.com/2015/06/28/upshot/in-an-uber-world-fortune-favors-the-freelancer.html.

DARLIN, DAMON. "Thinking of Rigging Your Home With Smart Devices? Start Here." *The New York Times*, 8 Mar. 2017, www.nytimes.com/2017/03/08/technology/personaltech/thinking-of-rigging-your-home-with-smart-devices-start-here.html.

DOUGHERTY, CONOR AND MIKE ISAAC. "Airbnb and Uber Mobilize Vast User Base to Sway Policy." *The New York Times*, 4 Nov. 2015, https://www.nytimes.com/2015/11/05/technology/airbnb-and-uber-mobilize-vast-user-base-to-sway-policy.html.

FORTIN, JACEY. "Richard Branson's Virgin and Hyperloop One Transit Pods Become Fast Friends." *The New York Times*, 12 Oct. 2017, www.nytimes.com/2017/10/12/business/virgin-richard-branson-hyperloop-one.html.

GREENHOUSE, STEVEN. "The Whatchamacallit Economy." *The New York Times*, 16 Dec. 2016, www.nytimes.com/2016/12/16/opinion/the-whatchamacallit-economy.html.

HARDY, QUENTIN. "Looking Beyond the Internet of Things." *The New York Times*, 21 Dec. 2017, www.nytimes.com/2016/01/02/technology/looking-beyond-the-internet-of-things.html.

IRWIN, NEIL. "Should the Fed Create 'FedCoin' to Rival Bitcoin? A Former Top Official Says 'Maybe'." *The New York Times*, 4 May 2018, www.nytimes.com/2018/05/04/upshot/should-the-fed-create-fedcoin-to-rival-bitcoin-a-former-top-official-says-maybe.html.

ISAAC, MIKE. "Airbnb Pledges to Work With Cities and Pay 'Fair Share' of

Taxes." *The New York Times*, 11 Nov. 2015, https://www.nytimes.com/2015/11/12/technology/airbnb-pledges-to-work-with-cities-and-pay-fair-share-of-taxes.html.

ISAAC, MIKE. "Uber Strikes Deal With Volvo to Bring Self-Driving Cars to Its Network." *The New York Times*, 20 Nov. 2017, www.nytimes.com/2017/11/20/technology/uber-deal-volvo-self-driving-cars-.html.

KAYSEN, RONDA. "Is My Not-So-Smart House Watching Me?" *The New York Times*, 27 Apr. 2018, www.nytimes.com/2018/04/27/realestate/is-my-not-so-smart-house-watching-me.html.

KRUPNICK, MATT. "Businesses Turn to Airbnb." *The New York Times*, 21 Dec. 2017, www.nytimes.com/2014/10/07/business/businesses-turn-to-airbnb-for-corporate-travel.html.

LANYADO, BENJI. "Europe Without Hotels." *The New York Times*, 15 July 2010, www.nytimes.com/2010/07/18/travel/18couch.html.

MILLER, STUART. "A Blockchain Building in Bushwick." *The New York Times*, 25 May 2018, www.nytimes.com/2018/05/25/realestate/a-blockchain-building-in-bushwick.html.

THE NEW YORK TIMES. "Full Tilt: When 100% of Cars Are Autonomous." *The New York Times*, 8 Nov. 2017, www.nytimes.com/interactive/2017/11/08/magazine/tech-design-autonomous-future-cars-100-percent-augmented-reality-policing.html.

PLUMER, BRAD. "When Will Electric Cars Go Mainstream? It May Be Sooner Than You Think." *The New York Times*, 8 July 2017, www.nytimes.com/2017/07/08/climate/electric-cars-batteries.html.

POLLACK, ANDREW. "A Powerful New Way to Edit DNA." *The New York Times*, 3 Mar. 2014, www.nytimes.com/2014/03/04/health/a-powerful-new-way-to-edit-dna.html.

POPPER, NATHANIEL. "Blockchain Will Be Theirs, Russian Spy Boasted at Conference." *The New York Times*, 29 Apr. 2018, www.nytimes.com/2018/04/29/technology/blockchain-iso-russian-spies.html.

POPPER, NATHANIEL. "A Former Top Wall Street Regulator Turns to the Blockchain." *The New York Times*, 22 Apr. 2018, www.nytimes.com/2018/04/22/technology/gensler-mit-blockchain.html.

POPPER, NATHANIEL. "What Is Bitcoin, and How Does It Work?" *The New York Times*, 1 Oct. 2017, www.nytimes.com/2017/10/01/technology/what-is-bitcoin-price.html.

QUAIN, JOHN R. "Self-Driving Cars Might Need Standards, but Whose?" *The*

New York Times, 23 Feb. 2017, www.nytimes.com/2017/02/23/automobiles/wheels/self-driving-cars-standards.html.

ROOSE, KEVIN. "Kodak's Dubious Cryptocurrency Gamble." *The New York Times*, 30 Jan. 2018, www.nytimes.com/2018/01/30/technology/kodak-blockchain-bitcoin.html.

SCOTT, MARK. "What Uber Can Learn From Airbnb's Global Expansion." *The New York Times*, 21 Dec. 2017, www.nytimes.com/2015/07/08/technology/what-uber-can-learn-from-airbnbs-global-expansion.html.

STREITFELD, DAVID. "Companies Built on Sharing Balk When It Comes to Regulators." *The New York Times*, 22 Apr. 2014, www.nytimes.com/2014/04/22/business/companies-built-on-sharing-balk-when-it-comes-to-regulators.html.

WADE, NICHOLAS. "Gene Drives Offer New Hope Against Diseases and Crop Pests." *The New York Times*, 21 Dec. 2015, www.nytimes.com/2015/12/22/science/gene-drives-offer-new-hope-against-diseases-and-crop-pests.html.

WAKABAYASHI, DAISUKE. "Self-Driving Uber Car Kills Pedestrian in Arizona, Where Robots Roam." *The New York Times*, 19 Mar. 2018, https://www.nytimes.com/2018/03/19/technology/uber-driverless-fatality.html.

WAKABAYASHI, DAISUKE. "Uber's Self-Driving Trucks Hit the Highway, but Not Local Roads." *The New York Times*, 6 Mar. 2018, www.nytimes.com/2018/03/06/technology/uber-self-driving-trucks.html.

WAYNE, TEDDY. "Grandpa Had a Pension. This Generation Has Cryptocurrency." *The New York Times*, 3 Aug. 2017, www.nytimes.com/2017/08/03/style/what-is-cryptocurrency.html.

WINGFIELD, NICK. "Amazon Buys Ring, Maker of Smart Home Products." *The New York Times*, 27 Feb. 2018, www.nytimes.com/2018/02/27/business/dealbook/amazon-buys-ring.html.

ZIMMER, CARL. "Scientists Find Form of Crispr Gene Editing With New Capabilities." *The New York Times*, 3 June 2016, www.nytimes.com/2016/06/04/science/rna-c2c2-gene-editing-dna-crispr.html.

ZITTRAIN, JONATHAN. "From Westworld to Best World for the Internet of Things." *The New York Times*, 3 June 2018, www.nytimes.com/2018/06/03/opinion/westworld-internet-of-things.html.

Index